What Every Client Needs to Know About Using a Lawyer

Other Books by Gregory White Smith and Steven Naifeh

Moving Up in Style
The Bargain Hunter's Guide to Art Collecting

Books by Steven Naifeh

Culture Making: Money, Success, and the New York Art World
Gene Davis

What Every Client Needs to Know About Using a Lawyer

Gregory White Smith
and
Steven Naifeh

G. P. Putnam's Sons
New York

Library of Congress Cataloging in Publication Data

Smith, Gregory White.
    What every client needs to know
about using a lawyer.

    Includes index.
    1. Attorney and client—United States.
I. Naifeh, Steven W., date.   II. Title.
KF311.S64   347.73'504   82-7524
ISBN 0-399-12761-5   347.3070504   AACR2

PRINTED IN THE UNITED STATES OF AMERICA

Acknowledgments

Our first words of thanks go to the many lawyers throughout the United States who permitted us to interview them for this book. Without their help, this book would not have been possible.

In particular, we want to thank our attorney Martin Leaf, who has not only set a consistently high standard for legal counsel but who graciously read the manuscript and made numerous helpful comments. Diane Acker, our classmate at law school and currently Professor of Law at Washburn University Law School in Topeka, Kansas, was also generous with her time, reading the manuscript and providing a detailed critique. We should quickly add, however, that any mistakes or errors of judgment that remain are strictly our own.

We are grateful to Robert Ambrose, who conducted the initial research for the book. Our thanks also to Deni Auclair, who edited the manuscript.

Connie Clausen, our agent, was her usual gracious and enthusiastic self. Our debt to her deserves more recognition than this limited space permits. Suffice it to say that she has been a friend, a challenge, and a constant joy. We also appreciate the assistance of her associate, Nancy Trichter, whose legal background was useful on several occasions. Finally, we are grateful to Faith Sale, our editor at G. P. Putnam's Sons. We especially appreciate the confidence she showed in us. That is a rare gift between editor and author in the publishing world, and we prize it greatly.

G.W.S.
S.N.
New York

To the Harvard Law School,
*where we learned that there are
no honorable professions,
only honorable people*

CONTENTS

1.
LEGAL SERVICES: A CONSUMER'S NIGHTMARE

Almost everyone feels, at some time, the frustrations of dealing with a lawyer. Everyone has heard the horror stories or lived through them. Surveys predict that almost 20,000,000 American adults will consult a lawyer in 1982, and, in many of those encounters, come away frustrated and resentful, convinced that it was the lawyer, and not the system, that "ripped them off."

Some people are so disenchanted with the quality and cost of legal services that they try to avoid lawyers altogether. They buy books about "being your own lawyer," form their own corporations, even represent themselves in court. The extremes to which some people will go to avoid lawyers is, perhaps, the most pointed proof that the legal profession has failed: failed in providing competent, affordable legal advice, failed in winning public confidence, and failed in making the principle of fair representation work.

The unfortunate but unavoidable fact is that lawyers, like doctors, *are* necessary. Many legal problems are just too complicated to be handled by laymen. Everyone has heard the old saying that the lawyer who represents himself has a fool for a client. But the same is true of the nonlawyer. Although there are times—many times—when you can get by without a lawyer, it would be unrealistic to assume that you'll never need professional legal advice. Life just isn't that simple.

This book is for that day you hope will never come but probably will: the day you really *need* a lawyer. When that day arrives, you'll need to know how to find a lawyer, how to work with a lawyer, how much to pay a lawyer, how to know if a lawyer's any good, and, if not, how to get rid of a lawyer. The answers are all here.

This book is also for lawyers. "A client's manual is a lawyer's manual too," says Martin Leaf, a highly respected New York lawyer. "It is a rare opportunity to look in the mirror, carefully and deeply, and see if you are all that you can be—all that you committed yourself to be when you became a lawyer."

THE MOST COMMON COMPLAINTS ABOUT LAWYERS

Almost everyone has a special gripe about lawyers and legal services. But there are some complaints that come up again and again in interviews with clients. One lawyer calls these the "litany of disgust." Undoubtedly you'll recognize some of these complaints from your own experience:
- Lawyers cost too much.
- Lawyers are incompetent.
- Lawyers are dishonest.
- Lawyers keep their clients in the dark.
- A good lawer is hard to find.

Lawyers Cost Too Much

- In 1977, when Chief Justice Walter McLaughlin retired from the Massachusetts Superior Court, he was asked what he considered to be the most pressing problem facing litigants. He answered without hesitation: "The fees. They're outrageous," he said. "With the cost of litigation these days, I think clients would often be better off if they just met in the halls and threw dice. Certainly it would be cheaper."

Legal services today are simply too expensive. Even when they're good, there's no strict correlation between quality and price. If there is a single factor that keeps people from using lawyers more often, it's the fear of ending up in the poorhouse. "People are scared," says Steve Arkans of the Legal Service Center of Arkans & Levin, a law clinic in Philadelphia. "They don't know what a lawyer's going to charge them." And they're afraid to ask.

Some lawyers are too embarrassed to tell people how much they make. James F. Neal, a Nashville attorney who achieved national recognition in the Watergate trials, says, "Frankly, I don't want to disclose my hourly rate. I'm embarrassed by hourly rates—not just mine, but everybody's." Other lawyers, however, are quick to defend fee levels. "The pressures are colossal," says New York attorney Norman Gutman in defense of the high fees he extracts. "I say to my clients that I give them slices of my life for which they can never repay me." The assumption, of course, is that a lawyer's life, not just his time, is worth more than other peoples'. Many clients would disagree.

Lawyers Are Incompetent

- A woman in Chicago hired a law firm to sue a taxi-cab company over an accident in which she was injured. Four years passed before her four lawyers realized that they were suing the wrong company.

Speaking before the American Bar Association in Dallas in 1979, Chief Justice Warren E. Burger estimated that between one-third and one-half of all the trial lawyers in the U.S. were not qualified to appear in a courtroom. He went on to decry "the ineptness, the bungling, the malpractice which can be observed in courthouses all over the country." Burger may be particularly outspoken in his pessimistic views of the legal profession's competence, but he's hardly alone. In a nationwide survey of federal judges, 41 percent said that incompetence among trial lawyers was a "serious" problem.

Lawyers Are Dishonest

- A highly distinguished lawyer and former president of the ABA was working for a client on an estate valued at $2,000,000. Despite regulations to the contrary, the lawyer made himself the beneficiary. He was subsequently disbarred by the very organization he once presided over.

Lawyers have suffered a bad press for a long time—with occasional exceptions. The French statesman Alexis de Tocqueville, for example, considered lawyers "the American aristocracy." But much more typical was the response of the English poet John Keats, who said, "I think we may class the lawyer in the natural history of monsters." And there was, of course, no place for lawyers in Thomas More's *Utopia*.

Lack of public respect for the legal profession has not changed with time. In fact, lawyers have never been in worse repute than during the last decade. Most people, lawyers and nonlawyers alike, tend to blame Watergate. Jerold S. Auerbach, a legal scholar and critic, says, "The long roster of Watergate lawyers convicted for obstruction of justice or perjury does not even include Richard Nixon, who, although pardoned by an alumnus of Yale Law School [Gerald Ford], was recently disbarred in New York."

But every abuse has a mitigating context. Watergate was a disease, no doubt, but it was also a purgation. Many of those who brought official abuses to light and prosecuted them were themselves lawyers. For every Richard Kleindienst there was an Archibald Cox; for every John Mitchell, a John Sirica.

Lawyers Keep Their Clients in the Dark

The reservoir of resentment against the legal profession is fed by ignorance as well as injury. Lawyers have traditionally considered law their private domain and resented any intrusions by nosy clients. "The guild mentality," says one legal critic, "survives in the paneled halls of law firms large and small." A recent *McCall's* survey revealed that a typical woman has three main complaints about her divorce lawyer: The lawyer "didn't spend enough time with me"; he "failed to advise me of my rights"; and "bullied me so I was afraid to disagree or ask questions." On almost any list of grievances against lawyers, "failure to communicate" is near the top.

Lawyers often try to respond to these complaints by arguing that a client wouldn't understand the legal issues anyway; and, besides, it takes too much time and effort to communicate in the "vernacular." Lawyers are not the sole targets of this indictment. Members of all the professions have invented special jargon to communicate more efficiently with each other—and less efficiently with outsiders. But no jargon is more *needlessly* complicated, pervasive, and impenetrable than legal jargon.

To use a typical legalism, the double negative, lawyers are "not unaware" of the problem. At the 1979 ABA meeting in Dallas, lawyers noted that "the American public is running out of patience with lawyers, and lawyers are running out of time." Gary C. Huckaby, a lawyer from Huntsville, Alabama, and a member of the ABA Task Force on Public Education, said, "We are not communicating with the public. We have got to demystify our business."

The trouble is, demystification goes against long-standing traditions—not only in the law but in all professions. Says economist Russell E. Palmer, "I'm afraid that many [professional] attitudes and practices have survived from a time when the consumer of professional services was often perceived as an ignorant and superstitious backwoodsman. It was thought best if he did not know what ailed him and safest if his prescriptions

were written in a language he couldn't read. If this characteriza-
tion ever had any basis, it has none now. There is, as the psychologist Leonard Neal says, 'a shortage of morons.'"

A Good Lawyer Is Hard to Find

In a 1978 survey, 82 percent of those responding agreed that
"a lot of people do not go to lawyers because they have no way
of knowing which lawyer is competent to handle their particular problem." Things haven't changed. Today, the accepted
wisdom among clients continues to be: "A bad lawyer is worse
than no lawyer at all."

Hard though it is to believe, there is no systematic, reliable
way to locate a good lawyer. In fact, even other *lawyers* have
trouble finding a good lawyer. A prominent New York enter-
tainment lawyer says, "When we need a lawyer in Michigan to
help us handle a case, we have nowhere to turn for a
recommendation. We can try looking in the *Harvard Law School
Alumni Directory* for a lawyer practicing in Michigan. But all
that tells us is that he went to a good school, it doesn't tell us
he's a good lawyer. Or we can try reading through the bios in
Martindale-Hubbell [the most exhaustive nationwide directory]
but that's like running your fingers through the Yellow Pages.
And the state lawyer referral services are worse than that: They
list all the *worst* lawyers."

Of course, if you already have a good lawyer—or a trustworthy friend who can put you in touch with a good lawyer—this
dilemma doesn't touch you. If you move, however, or are sued
in another state, or have a legal problem your present lawyer
can't handle, you may suddenly find yourself involved in an
unguided and time-consuming search for a good lawyer.

THE SEARCH FOR A GOOD LAWYER

After reading all about these problems with the legal profession, you may never want to walk into a lawyer's office again.

But don't be discouraged. For every incompetent, unethical, and overpriced lawyer, there are many competent, ethical, and affordable lawyers. With the right effort, good ones can be found.

Certainly there is no shortage of lawyers to choose from. Today, there are about 575,000 lawyers in the United States—50 percent more than a decade ago. And that number is still growing at a much faster rate than the population at large. The United States has always had a disproportionate number of lawyers compared with other countries. The ratio is now one lawyer for every 400 people compared to one for every 1,200 in England and one for every 8,000 in Japan.

In fact, the rule of supply and demand should begin to favor clients over time. Law schools, bloated by an 85 percent rise in enrollments between 1968 and 1978, are seeing more and more of their graduates join Ph.D.s in the ranks of the unemployed. Labor Department statistics estimate that by 1985, 100,000 lawyers—or one out of six—will be out of work.

Needless to say, that forbidding prospect has had a profound effect on the legal profession. Although the nation's leading corporate law firms still boast astronomical billing rates, even many of the best lawyers have responded to the laws of supply and demand by lowering fees to generate higher revenues through increased volume. The result is that, more and more, first-rate legal advice is becoming available at relatively low prices.

That's a very important development, since a good lawyer is one of the keys to good legal services. "It's like going into an operating room," says a lawyer in Chicago. "You have to put your faith in the surgeon's abilities."

WHAT THIS BOOK WILL DO FOR YOU

Another key to good legal services is a good client—one who works closely with his lawyer, who monitors his activities carefully, who knows what services he should be receiving and how much he should pay for them. "Behind every good lawyer," says a Boston attorney, "are good lawyer-client relationships. And behind every good lawyer-client relationship is a good client." This book will help make you the client you should be so your lawyer can be the lawyer he should be.

- It will help you determine if your lawyer is competent—and tell you what to do about it if he's not.
- It will help you determine if your lawyer is dishonest—and tell you what to do about it if he is.
- It will give you a guide to working with a lawyer—so that he can't keep you in the dark, even if he wants to.
- It will tell you how much to pay a lawyer—so that he can't get away with overcharging you.
- It will help you find a good lawyer in the first place—so you can avoid these problems altogether.
- And, if you're a lawyer, it will help you understand your clients' problems—so you can serve them better.

2.
DO YOU NEED A LAWYER?

Before we launch into lengthy descriptions of how to hire, supervise, pay, fire, and sue a lawyer, we ought to address the question of whether you *need* a lawyer in the first place. It is no novelty to find people doing their own legal work. It's always been possible to represent yourself in the legal system, although sometimes—if you're arguing before a court, for example—you have to get the court's permission.

What *is* new is the *popularity* of do-it-yourself legal work. More and more people are turning for legal advice to books, newsletters, and magazines in order to beat the high cost of lawyers. While there are, undoubtedly, many legal problems you can solve on your own or with a little help from books, there are also many too complicated or obscure for you to handle without expert help. The trick, of course, is to know which is which.

ALTERNATIVES TO HIRING A LAWYER

If you have a legal problem, a lawyer isn't necessarily the only person who can solve it. If you really want to avoid the cost of hiring a lawyer, consider the advantages and disadvantages of dealing with the problem in some other way. The most obvious alternative is to solve it on your own in a way that doesn't involve the law at all. The legal process is expensive and time-consuming—both to the litigants and to the taxpayers. If there's a way to settle a dispute without resorting to the legal system, you should explore it fully before you visit a lawyer—even before you buy a do-it-yourself kit. Don't add another spark to the "litigation explosion" unless you have to.

If you can't resolve the matter on your own, or if you need a question answered rather than a dispute resolved, there are still ways to avoid paying legal bills: Consult a nonlegal professional and/or take advantage of free legal information. Explore these alternatives thoroughly before paying a lawyer to explore them for you.

Consult a Nonlegal Professional

Doing without a lawyer doesn't have to mean doing it yourself; it can simply mean going to someone other than a lawyer for legal advice. In a 1978 ABA survey, over 80 percent of the respondents agreed that "there are many things that lawyers handle—for example, tax matters or estate planning—that can be done as well and less expensively by nonlawyers—like tax accountants, trust officers of banks, and insurance agents."

We agree. Many problems with legal ramifications can be resolved just as effectively, more quickly, and much more cheaply by someone other than a lawyer. There has long been a controversy, for instance, between the ABA and title insurance companies over who should handle real estate closings. The ABA says only a lawyer is capable of handling the legal work; the insurance companies insist they're capable of handling it themselves. The lawyers charge $50 per document; the insurance companies throw the service in as part of the deal. (Make sure the closing really is free, and isn't hidden somewhere in the paragraph on "closing costs.") Not all states have title insurance companies, but if yours does, and if your transaction is reasonably simple, you're obviously better off with the freebie.

One caution, however. Before you turn to a nonlawyer for legal advice, make sure that advice isn't tainted by self-interest. Insurance agents, for example, depend for their income entirely on selling insurance. If an agent gives you advice on some legal matter to the effect that you need more insurance, you should seek a second opinion.

Take Advantage of Free Information

The best time to turn to a nonlawyer for legal advice— assuming, of course, that he's competent—is when the non-lawyer doesn't charge for his services. But there are other ways of getting legal questions answered entirely free of charge.

If you have a legal question, begin by asking yourself what kind of question it is and whether there might be a public agency, a private foundation, or some other group that can answer it for you. Then simply call and ask. There's a wealth of free services available in this country that surprisingly few people bother to take advantage of. Here are some of the most frequently needed free resources:

- If you have a question about an insurance matter, call the office of your state's insurance commissioner, insurance department, or insurance bureau.
- If you have a question about welfare, call your local welfare office.
- If you have a question about social security, call your local social security office.
- If you have a question about a consumer product, call your state consumer protection agency or a private consumer protection group.
- If you have a question about a tax matter, call your local, state, or federal tax bureau or, for more "impartial" answers, a local taxpayers' association.

- If you have a question about a discrimination matter, call a state antidiscrimination commission or department, the nearest federal EEO (Equal Employment Opportunity) office, or the U.S. Attorney's Office. You may also appeal to the ACLU (American Civil Liberties Union), the NAACP (National Association for the Advancement of Colored People), NOW (National Organization of Women), or some similar group.
- If you have a question about a real estate matter, call your state real estate commission, a zoning commission, or a local tenants' association.
- If you have a question about a federal health or welfare program, call your local office of the Department of Health and Human Services.
- If you have a question involving state law, call the office of the state attorney general.
- If you have a question involving federal law, call the nearest regional branch of the U.S. Attorney's Office.
- If you have a question about the operations of the court (such as filing procedures, court dates, etc.), visit *(don't call)* the court clerk or other court official for the appropriate court.
- If you have any question about where to go with a question, call your local, state, or federal representatives. Few people realize that their elected representatives—especially in Washington—are well-equipped to answer a wide variety of questions.

Many public libraries have reference divisions where you can find answers to your questions. At the very least, they can often help lead you to some other source of information.

This is by no means an exhaustive listing, but it does give you some idea of the range of resources available. That trip to a lawyer's office may not be necessary after all. But even if it is, these sources of information—and many more like them—can serve as a useful and convenient way to check up on your lawyer's advice with a free second opinion.

DOING WITHOUT A LAWYER

There has recently been a barrage of books advocating legal self-help, arguing that people should fight the high cost and low quality of legal services by doing without lawyers altogether— or, more to the point, by doing it themselves. Books with titles such as *Without a Lawyer, Do You Need a Lawyer?*, and *How to Be Your Own Lawyer (Sometimes)* are only the most recent manifestation of public dissatisfaction with lawyers.

The American legal system does not require the use of a lawyer. Every citizen, lawyer and nonlawyer alike, is allowed to represent himself—to act *pro se* (on one's own behalf). But the important question isn't whether you *can* represent yourself; the question is whether you *should* represent yourself.

Sometimes the decision seems fairly clear. There are certain situations in which a lawyer's services are mandatory. If you're charged with a crime, you'd better get yourself a lawyer pronto. If, on the other hand, you want to collect an overdue debt in small claims court, a lawyer would probably do more to hinder your case than to help it.

Once you get beyond the obvious and easy examples, however, it's very difficult to get reliable, impartial advice on whether you need a lawyer for a particular problem. Not surprisingly, lawyers will tend to tell you that you need a lawyer. Richard Hinks, a Detroit lawyer who heads the ABA's panel on unauthorized legal practice, advises people not to use no-fault divorce kits unless there are no children and no property—a rare combination. Hinks also warns about the dangers of drawing up your own will: "It's the most important transaction in many people's lives—disposing of all their assets."

What if yours is not one of the easy cases? Whether you can

go it alone or should rely on a lawyer will depend on the facts of your particular case. To get an assessment of those facts, consult a lawyer. In general, large law firms will urge you not to use a lawyer in cases that can be handled without a lawyer's assistance. Smaller firms, because they see a prospective client, tend to overemphasize the need for a lawyer's advice. If you don't want to consult a lawyer, or if you doubt the impartiality of your lawyer's assessment, here are some questions to help you decide whether or not to be your own lawyer:

- Will you save money?
- How complicated is the law?
- How much time and effort will it take?
- How significant are the consequences?

Will You Save Money?

- Using a divorce-kit to save some money, a San Diego woman divorced her Marine Corps husband. She put together a settlement agreement on the basis of the instructions in the kit. Only much later—too late, in fact—did she discover that her husband's military pension was community property, and that it should have been included in the settlement. To save a few hundred dollars in legal fees, she lost half her husband's pension.

The main reason people try to do without a lawyer is to avoid paying a lawyer's fees. They consider every dollar not spent on a lawyer money in the bank. Unfortunately, it's not that simple. If you don't hire a lawyer, *somebody* has got to do the work, and chances are it will be you. Unless your situation is very unusual, your time is worth something and that something has to be deducted from the money you "save" by not paying a lawyer—and because you don't have any legal training, it may take you a lot more time than it would a lawyer.

If you handle your own case, you may miss something that a lawyer would catch. You might, for example, ask for less money than you could. Sometimes a lawyer's skills translate directly into money, and that's money you won't get if you go it alone. So, in order to decide if a do-it-yourself approach will *really* save you money, you need to answer some other questions.

How Complicated Is the Law?

Some cases are simpler than others—perhaps so much simpler that you can handle them yourself. Many books about being your own lawyer say that whether you can handle a case yourself is merely a matter of labels: divorce, yes; antitrust, no. In fact, labels are all but meaningless. It's the specific circumstances of your case that determine the matter.

Take wills, for example. If you own relatively little property, if you own that property outright, and if you want it all to go to your spouse, then you may want to buy a form and fill it out yourself. Of course, in even the simplest situation, you'll need to locate a safe place to put the will when it's completed and appoint an executor. You may also want to consider different ways to avoid probate altogether—no simple job, even with the help of a good self-help book.

Of course, if you own a substantial amount of property, much of which is mortgaged, and you want to split it up among several relatives, only a lawyer can ensure that the property ends up where you want it to go. A lawyer is even more indispensable if you want to make sure that as little as possible goes to the IRS.

To give you some idea of just how complicated the question of whether or not you can do it yourself can be, here is a list of factors that should be considered in determining if you need a lawyer to help you draw up a will. According to generally accepted principles, you need a lawyer if:

- your potential estate is worth more than $175,000, because the tax consequences become very complicated;
- you want to disinherit someone, because the will will probably be challenged if the person is a natural beneficiary;
- you have a beneficiary who needs special attention, for example, a child who is handicapped or mentally retarded;
- the property transactions upon your death will be complicated (if, for example, you own a small business and you want only one of your beneficiaries to inherit it).

How Much Time and Effort Will It Take?

Even if you're sure that your case is simple enough to handle without a lawyer, in almost every instance it will take you a lot longer than it would a good lawyer. An attorney in New Jersey says, "Trying a law suit without a lawyer will cost you money, even if it isn't in the form of cash. Preparing your case will take time. Then, when it goes to trial, you'll probably have to take time off from work. And time is money." If you consider your time valuable, then the time it takes to do your own research, draft your own documents, negotiate your own contracts, or argue your own case may be worth more to you than the cost of a lawyer.

You should also consider the added emotional costs of handling your own case. Divorce cases, for example, can take longer and cause more pain without the mediation and "buffer" that a good lawyer provides.

How Significant Are the Consequences?

We've saved the most important question for last: How much trouble can you get yourself into if you go it alone? If you make a mess of it, what's the worst that can happen? In a criminal case you should *always* have a lawyer because the consequences can be so grave: You stand a chance of losing your liberty—or your life—and not just your money. If it's a civil matter and "only" money is at stake, the critical question becomes: How much? Obviously, it wouldn't make any sense to pay a lawyer several hundred dollars to help you sue the corner cleaners for losing a $20 shirt. But what if they've lost two $100 suits? Then it might well be worth having a lawyer write a letter.

When Doing It Yourself Is Safest

In two kinds of cases, the general principle that you're better off using a lawyer than doing it yourself is reversed, primarily because the stakes are not high enough to warrant a professional's participation. The following are the safest instances in which you take your legal affairs into your own hands:

• *Small claims court.* Small claims courts exist in every state, and are designed so that individuals can represent themselves in cases involving relatively small amounts of money—usually less than $1,000. In fact, in some states individuals are prohibited from hiring lawyers to represent them in small claims courts. Ironically, they're considered detrimental to the efficiency and speed of these courts.

• *Traffic court.* Most traffic violations are not complicated enough, and the consequences not grave enough, to justify the attention or cost of a lawyer. If you don't already know it, call the court to find out the maximum fine for the violation. Unless the maximum fine is substantially greater than the cost of hiring a lawyer, or unless you are concerned about a violation appearing on your record, go it alone.

PRECAUTIONS TO KEEP IN MIND

Although the do-it-yourself ethic has its place even in the legal world, there are some facts you must know to be sure you don't make a major mistake:

• *The law differs from case to case.* Because self-help books deal only with general legal issues, they may not address the specifics of your case.

• *The law differs from state to state.* Only those self-help books directed to the citizens of your particular state will discuss the variations that apply in your own jurisdiction.

• *The law changes from day to day.* Because self-help books are written months or sometimes even years before they appear on the market, they're often out of date by the time they're published.

• *The law differs from court to court.* Professor Diane Acker of Washburn University Law School in Topeka, Kansas, says, "The law differs from judge to judge and court to court. No book can tell you about the judge's predilections or the court's procedural niceties."

Remember: If a lawyer bungles your case, you can sue him for malpractice (see Chapter 14); if you act as your own lawyer, you have no one to blame but yourself.

When to Bail Out

The do-it-yourself law books have done both a service and a disservice to the American public. They've demystified the law and shown clients that they can sometimes handle their own legal problems just as effectively—and much more cheaply— than a lawyer. But they've also helped create the impression that there's almost nothing a client can't do on his own, if he just has the right book. One unfortunate result is that people are tackling some legal problems that *should* be handled by a lawyer.

A smart man knows his limitations, even if he recognizes them late in the game. In the American legal system, it's almost never too late to run for cover. You can reach for a lawyer's help at any point in a case. If you have any reason whatsoever to think that you are not handling the case adequately yourself, by all means admit it and call in professional assistance. The real trick to handling your own legal affairs is knowing when you're in over your head.

HELP FOR DO-IT-YOURSELFERS

If you insist on cutting your own path through the legal jungle, you should at least be adequately prepared for it. Preparation is especially important if you decide to enter the courtroom unassisted. You don't have to go to law school, but you *do* have to do your homework. There are basically two things you ought to do:

• *Buy a book.* Literally dozens of self-help books have been published on the law, many of them quite good and available in most large libraries and bookstores. Here are some of the best:

Barry M. Gallagher, *How to Hire a Lawyer* (New York: Delta Books, 1979).

Philip Herman, *Do You Need a Lawyer?* (Englewood Cliffs, N.J.: Prentice-Hall, 1980).

Walter Kantrowitz and Howard Eisenberg, *How to Be Your Own Lawyer (Sometimes)* (New York: Perigee, 1979).

Samuel G. Kling, *The Complete Guide to Everyday Law*, third edition (New York: Jove Books, 1973).

Jane Shay Lynch and Sara Lyn Smith, *The Women's Guide to Legal Rights* (Chicago: Contemporary Books, 1979).

Joseph C. McGinn, *Lawyers: A Client's Manual* (Englewood Cliffs, N.J.: Prentice-Hall, 1979).

Burton Marks and Gerald Goldfarb, *Winning with Your Lawyer: What Every Client Should Know About How the Legal System Works* (New York: McGraw-Hill Book Company, 1980).

Steven Sarshik and Walter Szykitka, *Without a Lawyer* (New York: New American Library, 1980).

• *Get a kit.* In addition, there are several form books or "kits" to help you write a legal document or handle a legal problem. If you have any doubts about the reliability of these aides, you might refer to the 1976 *Yale Law Journal* study comparing divorces handled by divorce attorneys and those handled by spouses using do-it-yourself kits. The study found there was no significant difference in the number of errors made between the two groups. The following sources offer reliable kits:

HALT (Help Abolish Legal Tyranny; Suite 319, 201 Massachusetts Avenue, N.E., Washington, D.C. 20002) publishes a series of citizens' legal manuals: "Shopping for a Lawyer," "Real Estate," "Small Claims Courts," "Probate," and "Using a Law Library."

For people who want to incorporate their own small businesses or perform other simple corporate work, Ted Nicholas (Enterprise Publishing, Inc., Dept. AE-1XX, 725 Market Street, Wilmington, DE 19801) has written several useful self-help books: the best-selling *How To Form Your Own Corporation Without a Lawyer for Under $50*, *The Complete Book of Corporate Forms*, *How to Form Your Own Non-Profit Corporation Without a Lawyer for Under $75*, and *How to Form Your Own Professional Corporation*.

3.
WHAT KIND OF LAWYER DO YOU NEED?

"To treat a bar certificate of admission to practice law as a passport to try any and every kind of case in any court makes no more sense than to say a medical school degree qualifies the holder to perform any kind of surgery."

—Chief Justice Warren Burger

If you decide that you do need a lawyer, the next step is to find one. That should be simple enough in a society with more lawyers per capita than any other in the world. But, unfortunately, it's not. In fact, finding a lawyer can be an extremely complicated task. Why? Because you don't want just a good lawyer (one who's skilled, honest, and inexpensive), you also want the right *kind* of lawyer.

The legal profession is divided up into different "communities" of lawyers, each with its own strengths, skills, and clientele. Before you start looking for a competent, honest, and inexpensive lawyer, you should decide which of these communities is right for your legal business. Do you need a specialist or a general practitioner? Do you want a solo practitioner or a member of a large firm? Do you need the resources of a large firm or will those of a small firm be sufficient? Do you feel more comfortable working with a lawyer in a traditional law firm setting or should you take advantage of a legal clinic? Answering these questions carefully will narrow your search for the right lawyer to manageable proportions.

GENERAL PRACTITIONER OR SPECIALIST?

Lawyers, like doctors, are divided into two groups: generalists and specialists. A good general practitioner can handle most of the problems you're likely to run into, everything from incorporating a small business to selling a home. Martin Leaf, the New York attorney, calls them "people lawyers," because they "specialize" in the areas of law that touch most people's lives. They leave corporate mergers and securities law to others.

The specialists are lawyers who spend most of their time handling cases which involve one particular kind of issue or area of the law. They often—but not always—undergo special training. Usually their status as specialists rests on a combination of preference and extensive experience. They don't necessarily spend *all* their time working in their specialty, but, in order to lay a legitimate claim to the title, they should be spending at least 40 percent of their time doing specialized work.

Can a general practitioner handle your affairs or do you need a specialist? Unfortunately, there's no one answer to the question. If you already have a generalist for a lawyer, he should let you know when a specialist is required and continue to work with both you and the specialist. "I've never *lost* a client to a specialist," says attorney Leaf. "Rather, the specialist, the client, and I become partners in the effective, careful, and economical management of the 'specialized' problem."

Because not all lawyers are so cooperative, you should be prepared to decide for yourself if the services of a specialist are needed. Of course, if you don't already have a lawyer, you'll *have* to make the decision for yourself: to go first to a general practitioner and ask him if you need a specialist, or go straight to a specialist. Here are some questions to ask when deciding whether or not to go to a specialist:

- Does your state recognize specialties?
- Can you find a good generalist?
- Will a specialist cost more?
- What kind of case is it?
- What kind of specialist do you need?

Does Your State Recognize Specialties?

Professional specialization is a relatively recent development, and most state bar associations have been reluctant to recognize it. They prefer to think of the legal profession as a single, unified fraternity: A lawyer is a lawyer—not a tax lawyer, a divorce lawyer, or a criminal lawyer. Some state bar associations even prohibit lawyers from claiming a specialty. Some allow a lawyer to *designate* a particular field as a matter of preference. But only a few actually *certify* lawyers as specialists in particular fields. In fact, as of 1979, only California, Florida, Texas, and five other states required that a lawyer satisfy specific standards of education and experience before advertising himself as a specialist.

You should call your local or state bar association and ask what the recognized specialties in your state are and what a lawyer has to do in order to claim he's a specialist. Unless there are some requirements—such as passing an examination or taking supplementary courses—you may find that a "specialist in tax law" is really just someone who would like to handle more tax cases.

Can You Find a Good Generalist?

Surprisingly, a good general practitioner is harder to find than a good specialist. As in medicine, the talented people in law are often drawn to the intellectual challenges and higher fees of specialization. Because specialists tend to gravitate to big cities, finding a good generalist can be more difficult in the major metropolitan areas. Still, the search is well worth it. "New York has many excellent generalists," says one Manhattan attorney, "though not enough."

Will a Specialist Cost More?

The cost factor cuts both ways. As a rule, general practitioners charge less per hour than specialists—under the somewhat questionable assumption that general practitioners have less training, less experience, or less smarts than specialists. But because a specialist generally knows the area of law better than a generalist does, he supposedly needs less time to handle the problem. He will therefore bill you for fewer hours, making up the difference in billing rates. Theoretically, you end up paying the same total amount whether you go to a specialist or a generalist.

Unfortunately, it's not always that neat. In fact, you can pretty much rely on the fact that a specialist *will* cost you more than a generalist. What you're getting for the premium (in theory, at least) is better quality legal services.

There are exceptions to that rule. Just as there are general practitioners who know a remarkable amount about many areas of the law in which specialists know remarkably little, there are generalists who charge high rates and specialists who do not. The differences in cost between a specialist and a general practitioner depend less on the labels than on the level of each lawyer's skill and experience, his billing rate, and, above all, the complexity of your legal problem.

What Kind of Case Is It?

Questions such as whether your state recognizes specialists, whether you can find a good generalist, or whether a specialist will cost you more don't really determine your decision. Ultimately the decision to hire a specialist hinges on the nature of your particular case. As a rule, a general practitioner is perfectly capable of handling most problems in most areas. Only if your problem involves an unusually large sum of money or is unusually complex should you seek the assistance of a specialist.

• *Large sum of money.* If you have an estate worth less than $200,000 and you want to leave it entirely to your spouse or, if you should die simultaneously, to your children, any general practitioner should be able to make out the simple will required. On the other hand, if you have a large estate and you want to divide it up among several people in order to minimize inheritance taxes, you need the services of a skilled trusts and estates lawyer.

• *Complexity.* If you live in a state which permits no-fault divorces, if you have no children, and if your spouse is willing to agree in writing that you'll divide your property equally and that there will be no alimony, then a general practitioner is perfectly adequate. On the other hand, if you have children, you can't agree how to divide your property, or there's some dispute over alimony payments, you'd better find yourself a good divorce lawyer.

What Kind of Specialist Do You Need?

One of the hardest parts of finding a specialist is deciding which specialty your particular problem belongs to. The difficulty is compounded by the fact that most problems belong to more than one specialty. For example, if the IRS disputes the tax you pay on an inheritance and you have to go to court to defend yourself, do you have a tax problem (because it involves the IRS), a trusts and estates problem (because it involves a will), or a litigation problem (because you have to go to court)? Obviously, the answer is all three.

The fact that some problems seem to fall under more than one specialty is further complicated by legal terminology. It's often difficult to tell from the name of a specialty what kinds of problems fall under it. To help you see through the labels, here's a list of common legal problems and the appropriate specialists for dealing with them. The list, although by no means exhaustive, should steer you in the right direction.

A GUIDE FOR MATCHING LEGAL PROBLEMS WITH LEGAL SPECIALISTS

You need a domestic relations lawyer if:
    you want to file for a divorce;
    you want to resolve a marital dispute;
    you want to write a prenuptial agreement;
    you want to adopt a child;
    you want to enforce a child custody and support agreement;
    you want to collect delinquent alimony payments;
    you want to stop paying alimony;
    you want a divorce settlement.

You need a criminal defense lawyer if:
    you've been notified to appear before a grand jury;
    you've been notified of an investigation that involves you;
    you've been detained for shoplifting;
    you've been accused of any criminal offense;
    you've been arrested.

You need a real estate lawyer if:
    you want to fight an eviction order;
    you want to dislodge an unwanted tenant;
    you want to buy or sell a piece of land, house, condominium, or cooperative apartment;
    you want to negotiate a lease;
    you want to get out of an unfavorable lease.

You need a business lawyer if:
    you want to set up a small business;
    you are buying or selling a business;

you are thinking of investing in a business venture;
you have a complicated commercial transaction.

You need a bankruptcy lawyer if:
you want to declare bankruptcy;
you find that someone has filed an involuntary bankruptcy
action against you;
you have been notified that someone who owes you money
has filed for bankruptcy.

You need a litigation lawyer if:
you want to challenge a school disciplinary measure;
you've been discriminated against in employment;
you want to dispute a credit rating;
you want to collect an overdue debt;
you're the victim of a sexual assault;
you want to sue trespassers for damage;
you want to sue anyone for anything;
you've been sued by anyone for anything.

You need a products liability litigation lawyer if:
you want to sue the manufacturer of a defective product.

You need a personal injury litigation lawyer if:
you want to sue someone for a personal injury;
you want to dispute a personal injury claim.

You need a malpractice litigation lawyer if:
you want to sue a physician for malpractice;
you want to sue a lawyer.

You need a copyright and patent lawyer if:
you want to copyright something you've written or music
you've composed;
you want to patent an invention.

You need a trusts and estates lawyer if:
    you want to write a complex will;
    you want to contest a will;
    you want to avoid probate;
    you want to set up a trust;
    you want to plan your estate.

You need a tax lawyer if:
    you want to dispute an IRS assessment;
    you want to shelter some of your income;
    you want to transfer assets to your children or spouse.

You need an immigration lawyer if:
    you want to take out U.S. citizenship;
    you want to extend a student visa;
    you want to fight deportation proceedings.

The abundance of legal specialties can be overwhelming to a potential client. Before it was disbanded, the Standing Committee on Law Lists of the American Bar Association put together a list of no less than 159 legitimate specialties.

LARGE FIRM OR SMALL?

Law firms come in all sizes: from the small-town, storefront solo practitioner who works alone, often without even a secretary, to Chicago's mammoth Baker & McKenzie with six hundred lawyers, in addition to paralegals, administrators, clerks, secretaries, receptionists, librarians, and messengers.

Of course, chances are very good that you'll end up with neither a solo practitioner nor a behemoth like Baker & McKenzie. Most firms in this country range in size from three or four lawyers to thirty or forty.

Just because one firm has more lawyers than another doesn't mean it handles more specialties. In fact, if anything, the opposite seems more often to be true. Although only some small firms specialize (restricting their practices to bankruptcy, say, or domestic relations), *most* large firms limit their practices to corporate law, securities, antitrust, business litigation, real estate, tax, trusts and estates, and related fields. The firms with the most general practice average five to ten lawyers and often handle everything from business counseling to divorce settlements.

The size of the firm you go to may have less to do with the nature of your legal problems than with the size of the town you live in. In most parts of the country, a firm with ten lawyers is considered medium-size, one with sixty lawyers, very large. However, in New York, Chicago, Houston, Los Angeles, or San Francisco, a firm with ten lawyers is tiny and one with sixty lawyers is medium-size. In those large cities, a very large firm is one with two hundred lawyers.

What are the advantages and disadvantages of size? When is a large firm better than a small firm? What size is right for your legal business? Beyond the obvious, cosmetic differences—large firms generally have more impressive addresses, better furnishings, more secretaries and paralegals—what are the differences that really count?

Advantages of a Small Firm

• *Cost.* As a general rule, lawyers in small firms charge less than lawyers in big firms. Because small firms don't usually have prestigious addresses, fancy offices, and extensive support staffs, they don't have the high overhead costs that are typical of large firms. Moreover, because the lawyers in small firms generally pay themselves less, they can generally charge clients less.

• *Concern.* Lawyers in small firms are like family doctors. They're friends and counselors first, attorneys second. When you go to them with a problem, they'll take a personal interest. Large firms, by contrast, are factories: Yours is just one of a thousand cases. Even worse, lawyers in large firms rarely deal with their actual clients, the corporations they represent; they deal with corporate officers. It's hard to develop concern, compassion, or any sort of personal connection when you work with IBM or DuPont all day.

• *Convenience.* As we stated earlier, some people don't have the luxury of a choice between a small firm and a large one. In most parts of the country, the largest firm in the neighborhood probably has only three or four lawyers. Therefore, if you want a lawyer who's close to home, the choice between a small firm and a large one may be made for you.

Advantages of a Large Firm

• *Specialization.* In a large firm, if you need a specialist, your regular lawyer can just call someone down the hall. In a small firm, your lawyer may have to recommend that you go elsewhere—a hard thing for many lawyers to do. And if your lawyer doesn't recommend somebody specifically, you face the problem of finding a competent lawyer all over again. The greatest danger, of course, is that he may try to handle the case himself even though he lacks the necessary expertise. Early in 1981, the California Supreme Court put a solo practitioner on probation for one year for trying to handle a probate case without the proper qualifications.

• *Resources.* Addresses, furnishings, and receptionists are window dressing. Libraries, researchers, and research facilities, however, are important resources that could directly affect the outcome of your case. A lawyer in a small firm may have to travel some distance to a courthouse library to research your problem; a lawyer in a large firm has only to walk down the hall. The lawyer saves time and you save money. But most important, when the library is convenient, your lawyer won't hesitate to use it.

Research personnel are also a prime resource. A lawyer in a small firm has to do more of the work himself. One in a large firm has access to messengers, paralegals, and secretaries—day or night, if necessary. This can lower your costs (assuming the lawyer is honest enough to bill you at the lower staff rate) and insure that your urgent problems are handled quickly.

• *Continuity.* If your solo practitioner lawyer takes a long vacation, gets sick, or dies, you don't have a lawyer. Allen Zerfoss, the chief of lawyer discipline for the Pennsylvania bar, says: "If the lawyer gets sick or becomes an alcoholic, he has no one to fall back on, so he falls behind, misses court dates and gets into trouble." If the same thing happens to a member of a large firm, there's always a colleague around who can substitute while your lawyer is out or incapacitated. Most clients find it very reassuring to know that there is always someone to talk to.

• *Solvency.* If the worst happens and you have to sue your lawyer for malpractice, your chances of getting a satisfactory settlement or recovery from a sizeable firm are much better than they are if your lawyer practices solo. Large firms are more likely to have adequate malpractice insurance, and are therefore also more likely to have the money to pay the judgment.

• *Other offices.* Some large firms have offices in more than one state—some in more than one country. Baker & McKenzie has twenty-eight offices worldwide. Obviously, a law firm with offices in more than one jurisdiction is especially useful if you have legal business in more than one jurisdiction: It saves you the trouble of finding a local lawyer every time you have a legal problem outside your state.

It is sometimes possible to enjoy the benefits of offices in other jurisdictions without turning to a large firm. Some small firms maintain close associations with firms in other states and even other countries. Such liaisons are not rare, but you should ask in advance if you think you may need one.

Deciding Which Is Right for You

In deciding whether to go to a large or a small firm, you should keep in mind that there are no hard-and-fast rules. While most small firms charge less than large ones, some charge considerably more. For example, Melvin Belli, the famous personal injury lawyer, heads a firm with only ten lawyers, yet he charges some of the highest rates in the profession.

Generally speaking, the size of the firm you choose should reflect the nature of your legal problems. If you own a sizeable business and you're willing to spend the premium for the efficiency, specialized talents, and ample resources of a large firm, look for a good lawyer in a large firm. On the other hand, if your legal problems are more typical—you occasionally have a house to sell, a will to write, an insurance claim to settle—find a good lawyer in a small firm and enjoy the savings.

Ultimately, however, the individual lawyer is more important than the size of the firm. If you trust your lawyer and are comfortable working with him, it doesn't matter if he's in a firm of two or two hundred.

TRADITIONAL LAW FIRM OR LEGAL CLINIC?

Before the Supreme Court's 1975 decision which struck down as unconstitutional the Bar Association's ban on advertising, there were perhaps thirty legal clinics in the entire United States—most of them just barely surviving. "Today," says Davida Maron, formerly of the National Resource Center for Consumers of Legal Services, "we can't keep track of how many there are. New ones spring up every day."

The simplicity of the concept is largely responsible for its success: Set up shop in a plain building in a busy shopping area, forget the frills and the fancy decoration, offer only the most basic services in the areas people need most, standardize the procedures, use low-cost nonlawyers to do as much of the work as possible, leave the complex litigation to others, offer pre-established fees, and advertise like crazy. As Jane Bryant Quinn wrote in *Newsweek*, "Young lawyers dream of doing for their profession what H & R Block did for tax preparing and McDonald's did for hamburgers: standardize the product and deliver it in volume."

In fact, there are now approximately 2,000 legal clinics in the United States. The exact figure is hard to come up with because there's no precise definition of what constitutes a legal clinic. The word "clinic," borrowed from the medical profession, conjures up images of a staff of professionals "treating" a waiting room full of assorted problems. Yet many "clinics" are nothing more than a single lawyer with, perhaps, a secretary who doubles as a paralegal. Because there are no standards, one man's solo practitioner is another man's legal clinic.

The new competitive spirit and the lower prices generated by the boom in legal clinics have been especially effective in attracting middle-income clients who previously might have gone without legal services. Frederick Young Campbell, a Los Angeles attorney, says the people responding to his advertisements are "middle- and lower-middle-class people who don't qualify for legal aid and have a horror of walking into a lawyer's office, even when they have big legal problems. They expect they'll have to lay $500 on the table right off."

So, if you're inclined to think a lawyer is beyond your financial means, you're probably the right kind of client for a legal clinic. And if you've used lawyers in the past, but felt you were paying more than you should, a clinic may be the right compromise.

If you're thinking of taking your legal business to a legal clinic, you should keep in mind that the lawyer is more important than the kind of organization he belongs to. There are, however, certain common characteristics of legal clinics which make them better suited to perform certain legal tasks and less well suited to perform others. While most offer competitive prices and good customer service, they are also prone to erratic quality, erratic prices, and erratic ethics.

Advantages of Legal Clinics

• *Competitive prices.* The primary advantage of legal clinics is that they're not above price competition. Unlike conventional lawyers and conventional law firms—both large and small—

legal clinics are more inclined to advertise and more inclined to undercut prevailing prices for particular services. The result is a model of the free market: Prices are down and volume is up. The Law Store in Los Angeles, for example, has a legal information telephone service. For a mere $9.95 you can call an attorney, billing the charges to your credit card.

Just how cheap are legal clinics? Here are the fees (minus court costs) charged for some common legal procedures by clinics in different parts of the country in 1980:

Initial Consultation	*Uncontested Divorce*	*Simple Incorporation*	*Adoption*
New York (Jacoby & Meyers)			
$20	$225	$175	$360
Chicago (Jerold E. Slutzky & Associates)			
Free	$200	$300	$300+
New Orleans (The Legal Clinics of Paul Perrone)			
$15	$200	$250	$200-$300
Dallas (The Legal Clinic of Young & White)			
$15	$150	$150	$250
New York, District of Columbia, Maryland, and Tennessee (The Legal Clinic of Cawley & Schmidt)			
Free	$150	$175	$100-$175
Tampa (The Family Legal Clinics of Thomas J. Chawk)			
Free	$75	$100	$100
Phoenix (O'Steen Legal Clinic)			
$15	$150	$200	$225

• *Customer service.* The best legal clinics have managed to cut costs without cutting quality and their customers tend to come away satisfied. In 1979, the *American Bar Journal* conducted a survey of consumers in Los Angeles to learn how clients react to legal clinics as opposed to more traditional law firms. According to the survey, clinics scored better than firms in each of the seven categories researched:

• acting promptly;
• demonstrating interest and concern;
• dealing honestly with clients;
• explaining matters fully;
• keeping clients informed;
• paying attention to what clients have to say;
• charging fair and reasonable prices.

Disadvantages of Legal Clinics

• *Erratic quality.* The quality of legal services available varies unpredictably from one lawyer to the next. You can get first-rate service from a solo practitioner and terrible service from a large, prestigious firm. Erratic quality is a problem throughout the legal profession, and unless your case is routine, it can be especially acute among legal clinics.

• *Erratic prices.* Despite the low advertised rates, legal clinics can be expensive if they can't use standard procedures to deal with your case. Betsy Stark, a reporter for *The American Lawyer*, recently tested nine different legal clinics. In each case, she told the lawyer that she had taken an heirloom wedding band to a jeweler to have it sized for her own marriage. When she went to pick up the ring, the jeweler told her that he had mistakenly sold it to another customer. Stark took the fabricated case to all nine legal clinics. The suggested procedures and estimated fees ranged, incredibly, from $45 to $2,122. The higher figure was at least as much as a Wall Street firm would have charged if it had been willing to take the case.

• *Erratic ethics.* "Lawyers at some of the clinics," Stark

reports, "were absolutely scrupulous, even going so far as to offer free help. Others were lazy or seemed ready to overcharge, and the man who wanted to charge the least claimed to be a lawyer but is not registered with the New York State Bar." Stephen Brill, editor of *The American Lawyer*, notes that "many [clinics] handle nonroutine cases so badly and so expensively as to constitute consumer frauds, and . . . as with everything else in life, their standards of service and ethics vary."

Deciding Which Is Right for You

There's no reason not to use legal clinics, as long as you use them to serve a purpose they were originally *intended* to serve. If the answer to each of the following questions is yes, then you should seriously consider the option of a legal clinic, especially if you'd like to cut the cost of legal services:

- Is the legal service you require routine?
- Is the charge for the service lower than a conventional firm would charge?
- Are the charges in writing?
- Are you sure there are no hidden costs?
- Is it unlikely that the service will require hourly work?
- Is the clinic lawyer's hourly rate less than that of a lawyer in a conventional firm?

4.
HOW TO FIND A LAWYER

There are more than 575,000 lawyers in America. Some are experienced, skilled, ethical professionals; some are inexperienced, incompetent, unethical amateurs. Some charge reasonable prices, some charge obscene prices. Some have general practices that are of use to almost everyone, some have specialties so narrow they're of use to almost no one. In this maze of legal services, it's dangerously easy for the consumer to get lost.

Ultimately, the search for adequate legal service is a search for the right lawyer. If you have the right lawyer, everything else should fall into place. This chapter is about that search; Where do you look for a good lawyer and how do you know when you've found one?

A STEP-BY-STEP GUIDE TO FINDING THE RIGHT LAWYER

It's easy to find a good lawyer if you know the right people. Melvin Belli gives this advice to people looking for a lawyer:

"First, get a consensus [about a particular lawyer] from talking with newspaper people you may know, some judges you know—the people who move the community. Then go to him personally, and see how you get along. If you don't think you could work with him, then get the hell out of there."

That sounds simple enough. But the process of finding the right lawyer is not easy for most people. They may not happen to know journalists, judges, and the other "people who move the community." They usually don't even know any other attorneys. For most people, the search for a lawyer is a search from scratch.

If this is your predicament, finding the right lawyer may take some extra time and effort, but the results will be well worth the trouble. Here is a three-step method to help you in your search.

Step One: Assemble a List of Candidates

The first step in finding the right lawyer is to narrow the field. After you've decided what kind of lawyer you need (see Chapter 3), you should put together a list of candidates who satisfy your basic criteria (e.g., solo practitioner, specialist, convenient location, moderate prices, etc.). There's a variety of sources you can use to assemble this initial list: the recommendations of friends and relatives, referral services, lawyers and other professionals, advertisements, legal directories, and the Yellow Pages. These sources, and their strengths and weaknesses, are discussed below. The process of assembling a list of candidates can be long and tedious, but you should resist the temptation to forego it and rely on one source alone—no matter how good you think that source is.

Step Two: Narrow the List of Candidates

Once you have a list of candidates, you need to cross-check it. For example, if you've gotten the name of a tax lawyer from a friend, check out the recommendation with an accountant or with a lawyer in another field. If you were given the name of a divorce lawyer by a referral service, call a marriage counselor or family court judge. If you've gotten the name of a real estate lawyer from an advertisement, call the local real estate board, an agent who's a friend, or someone who teaches real estate law at a nearby law school. In every case, you should look the lawyer's name up in a published directory such as *Martindale-Hubbell*, read his biography, and note his background, education, clients, and peer rating.

Step Three: Visit the Remaining Candidates

Finally—and this is crucial— you should check out personally the lawyers remaining on your list. The riskiest thing a client can do is to accept a lawyer on faith. The foundation of a good lawyer-client relationship is compatibility and all the recommendations in the world can't guarantee that you will get along; only a personal encounter can do that. Of course, interviewing is time-consuming, but if you have cross-checked your list of candidates thoroughly, you should have only a few lawyers—five, perhaps—whom you want to interview. These interviews are usually free (though not always) and the time you spend on them may well save you the enormous expense in time, money, and anxiety of dealing with incompetent legal counsel at a later date. Once you've made an appointment with your "finalists," be sure to plan the interview in advance. (See Chapter 5, "Choosing a Lawyer," for some suggestions on asking the right "hard" questions.)

This three-step process may seem long and tedious, especially if you're one of the many people who usually just "let their fingers do the walking" when they need someone to do a job for them. Do you really need to go to all this trouble if all you want is a lawyer to draw up a simple will? Just how thorough do you *need* to be in looking for a lawyer? The answer depends on three things: how complicated your legal business is; how much money is at stake; and, ultimately, how much you care about your case.

For example, it's unlikely that a lawyer will make a major mistake incorporating a small business. And if he does, the consequences aren't particularly grave. Therefore, choosing a lawyer to do your incorporation shouldn't require a full-scale, month-long search. Any reasonably competent and honest lawyer should suffice. On the other hand, if you're charged with manslaughter or sued for divorce, there are countless ways that a lawyer could bungle your defense and cause you serious damage. The more serious the consequences of bad legal advice, the more thorough your search to avoid it should be.

WHERE TO LOOK FOR CANDIDATES

There are many sources from which to draw up your preliminary list of lawyers: friends and relatives, lawyers and other professionals, referral services, lawyers' advertisements, standard legal directories, even the Yellow Pages. Here are some points to keep in mind concerning each of these potential sources.

Friends and Relatives

Most people looking for a lawyer start by asking friends and relatives for recommendations. This is by far the most popular way of finding a lawyer, and also, unfortunately, the riskiest. Of course, if your friend or relative happens to be a lawyer, or is well connected in the legal community, the referral can be very useful. But no matter how well-informed the recommendation might be, you should never rely on it alone. Friends and relatives are a good place to *start* your search for a lawyer, but they're a bad place to end it.

There is, however, a little-recognized advantage to using a

lawyer recommended by a friend or relative that you should be aware of. If your recommendation comes from one of a lawyer's best clients, that lawyer may give you exceptionally good service and/or reduced fees in order to please his client. For example, if you work for a large company and need a tax lawyer, you should ask your company's in-house counsel for the name of a lawyer your company uses (or someone in the lawyer's firm). You'll probably find that lawyer willing to be very helpful in order to preserve his firm's reputation with your company. It's not unusual for small clients to ride on the coattails of big clients this way, and thereby enjoy the same attentive service.

Despite such occasional advantages, you should always treat the recommendations of friends and relatives with some skepticism. Here are several reasons why:

• *People like to make recommendations.* It gives them a sense of power. Lawyers know that, and tend to give those clients who regularly bring in new clients better service than they give the new clients. Using such recommendations will give your friend's ego a boost—and the lawyer's billings a boost—but it may not answer your own needs.

• *Some lawyers provide a kickback to people who bring in new clients.* Bail bondsmen, for example, are notorious for taking a substantial kickback—sometimes as much as 25 percent of the fee—from the lawyers they send clients to. Lawyers also sometimes split their fees with other lawyers who send them clients. It's illegal to take part of a lawyer's fee without doing part of his work, but that doesn't keep people from doing it. Be sure to ask a lawyer if he'll receive a fee for his recommendation.

• *Your friends and relatives probably have no more to base a recommendation on than you do.* Even if a friend has used a lawyer, he doesn't necessarily have any better means of evaluating the lawyer's services than you do. "[The lawyer] may have been adequate or inadequate," says New York divorce attorney Raoul Felder. "The friend has no way to judge." Another friend might tell you that a lawyer is a good lawyer when what he really means is that the lawyer is a nice person.

If you do want to shop around among friends and relatives for the name of a lawyer, be sure to protect yourself. Learn to distinguish the good recommendations from the bad by asking the right questions. For example:

- How did they hear of the lawyer in the first place? Was it from a reputable source—or merely from another branch of the grapevine?
- Did they actually hire the lawyer themselves, and if so was it for a case similar to yours?
- Were they satisfied with the lawyer's professional conduct—and with the results?
- How much did the legal work cost them? Were there any disputes over fees?

Referral Services

For almost four decades, many local bar associations have administered referral services to help put clients and lawyers together. Unfortunately, the quality of these services varies considerably. Some make a conscientious attempt to furnish the name of an appropriate lawyer; some merely furnish a name. In order to know how reliable a referral from one of these services is, you have to be able to evaluate the service itself. Here are some questions to ask:

- What kind of lawyer will you be referred to?
- Does the lawyer have a right to refuse your case?
- How is the referral service paid?
- Why do lawyers join the referral service?

• *What kind of lawyer will you be referred to?* The main problem with lawyer referral services is the kind of lawyers they refer you to. Some referral services make no attempt whatsoever to match the client up with a lawyer who specializes in the appropriate area of law. They just keep lists of lawyers and give out names on a rotating basis: Whichever name happens to be at the top of the list is the name you get. "In their effort to be fair," says Edward Bennett Williams, "they just go down the list. They don't even begin to evaluate the talents, abilities and competence of a lawyer."

• *Does the lawyer have a right to refuse your case?* Many lawyer referral services require that participating attorneys accept *all* clients referred to them by the service. They can refuse to represent a client only if they can prove that there's an ethical or personal reason for doing so, or that they lack the appropriate qualifications. Why would a good lawyer with a thriving practice be willing to give up his right to accept or deny a client?

• *How is the referral service paid?* Many referral services charge the client a flat fee for a referral, usually between $10 and $15. But they also charge the *lawyer* a fee (from as little as the $10 charged by the Rockland County Bar service in New City, New York, to as much as the one-third of the fees over $250 charged by the Hudson County Bar service in Jersey City, New Jersey). Again, you should ask yourself, why would a good lawyer with a good practice be willing to split his fees with a referral service?

• *Why do lawyers join the referral service?* The logical inference is that the only lawyers who join referral services are lawyers who lack clients. In general, the inference is valid. And, in general, they lack clients either because they're inexperienced or because they're incompetent. In fact, the ABA's *Statement of Standards and Practices for a Lawyer Referral Service* says that "sympathetic consideration should be given to the registration of recently admitted and less experienced lawyers."

Of course, the ABA doesn't recommend that sympathetic

consideration be given to *incompetent* lawyers, but most referral services don't impose very strict criteria for membership. In many cases, the only real criterion is the number of years the lawyer has practiced.

Either way—inexperienced or incompetent—the lawyers recommended by lawyers' referral services are rarely the best in the community—the kind of lawyers, in other words, that you're looking for. In fact, these services are even less reliable than the Yellow Pages for finding a lawyer. Even without intending it, they often screen *out* the best lawyers.

To give them their due, we should say that some referral services make a good-faith effort to refer you to a competent lawyer with the appropriate specialty. The Lawyer Referral Service of Philadelphia, for example, has a staff of five hundred lawyers on call. For a nominal registration fee, a paralegal or staff attorney will help the client determine the nature of his legal problem and, occasionally, solve it on the spot. If not, the staff lawyer has learned enough in this brief first meeting to make an educated referral to an appropriate lawyer. For $15, the client gets a valuable referral and a half-hour consultation with the staff attorney thrown in at no extra charge.

Here are some additional questions you can ask, depending on your needs, to decide how good the referral services in your area are:

- Do they have an in-house legal staff to provide legal service on simple matters?
- Is there a lawyer in charge of the advice?
- Do they have special panels for specialties of particular concern to the community, such as immigration law, military law, poverty law or juvenile law?
- Do they require that a lawyer have a certain amount of experience before they'll add his name to their referral lists?
- Do they keep records of the lawyers' areas of specialty in order to match clients with suitable lawyers?

- Do they try to make referrals according to the geographical convenience of the client?
- Do they make any special provisions for handicapped clients?
- Do they inform potential clients of the cost of an initial consultation (though never the estimated costs of representation)?
- Do they solicit comments from clients on the quality of the services provided?
- Do they have peer review boards?
- Do they permit nonlawyers on lawyer referral service committees or supervisory panels?
- Do they offer compulsory arbitration procedures in the event a dispute arises between lawyer and client?
- Do they have disciplinary boards to investigate the ethical conduct of attorneys?
- Do they require that participating lawyers take out malpractice insurance in order to protect clients?

When you call your local lawyer referral service, simply ask whether the service offers these assurances. Or, better yet, write the Standing Committee on Lawyer Referral Services of the American Bar Association (1155 East Sixtieth Street, Chicago, Illinois 60637) for a copy of its *Reference Handbook*. No lawyer referral service offers all of these assurances and only a few offer the most important ones, such as careful screening of candidates and compulsory arbitration. But the more assurances your local service offers, the more you can trust its referrals.

As an added precaution, be sure to get more than one name—then investigate each candidate's credentials on your own. If the referral service refuses to give you more than one name, call back a few days later and make the same request.

Lawyers and Other Professionals

If you want to find a lawyer by word of mouth, you should try to get the word from the right mouth. A recommendation from someone who has the expertise to assess a lawyer's competence is much more valuable than the rave reviews of a neighbor or fellow worker. Good sources of *informed* referrals are other lawyers, law school professors, judges and other courtroom personnel, and other professionals ranging from accountants to bankers to physicians, depending on the nature of your case and the specialty of the lawyer you're looking for.

Obviously, you should try to form some independent judgment of the recommender's reliability. Just because an accountant is an accountant doesn't mean he knows the best tax lawyers in your area. In fact, all professionals tend to stratify along the same levels of competence: Good accountants tend to know good lawyers, bad accountants tend to know bad lawyers. You should also find out how the recommender knows the lawyer being recommended. If they play golf together at the local country club, don't rely too heavily on the recommendation.

• *Other lawyers.* Edward Bennett Williams, the criminal lawyer, says, "It's always safest to be referred by a lawyer to another lawyer who will have some expertise for the client's particular needs." Lawyers can be helpful indeed, but don't count on it. Some of the best corporate lawyers don't have any idea who the best divorce lawyers or criminal lawyers in their area are. Asked for a recommendation, they may give you the first name that comes to mind. General practitioners, in contrast, often know a great deal about the specialists individual clients need most. But even their recommendations should never be accepted without further checking.

• *Law school professors.* One of the best—and one of the least used—ways to find a lawyer is to ask a professor at a local law school. Because they're often active in the local legal community, law school professors tend to know many of the best lawyers in the local bar—especially in their area of specialization. And because they usually don't engage in much practice themselves, their recommendations are relatively unbiased.

If you don't think a professor will bother to give you a recommendation, consider the following. In 1977, a reporter from *Consumer Reports* called five law schools in the New York area. At each school she called the dean's office or the public information office, said she was looking for a divorce lawyer, and asked for the name of a professor who specialized in family law. At four of the five schools, she was given the name of an appropriate professor, and in each case the professor gladly provided her with a referral. Two even encouraged her to call again if the referral turned out to be inadequate.

• *Judges and other courtroom officials.* If you need a litigator, either civil or criminal, it makes sense to ask an impartial observer who has an opportunity to see litigators at work in the courtroom: a judge. Previously published guides on how to find a lawyer state that some judges will make recommendations, even to complete strangers. Our experience suggests the contrary. Most judges feel that recommending one lawyer over another is a violation of judicial impartiality.

Of course, if you know a judge personally, or if you can find one who will make recommendations, by all means take advantage of this. If a judge won't help, however, ask other courtroom personnel. Although a judge has a good opportunity to assess the abilities of the lawyers who appear in his courtroom, so do the prosecuting attorneys, courtroom clerks, marshals, and stenographers.

• *Other professionals.* Among the best sources for names of lawyers in particular specialties are other professionals who work in related areas. (As always, the professional should be consulted only if you have good reason to trust his judgment and if he's a disinterested party.) The following are likely sources of referrals:

- If you need a tax lawyer, a trusts and estates lawyer, or a business lawyer: ask a bank officer, a stockbroker, an accountant, a tax counselor, or a financial executive.
- If you need a real estate lawyer: ask a real estate agent.
- If you need a personal injury lawyer: ask an insurance agent.
- If you need a domestic relations lawyer: ask a marriage

counselor, a psychologist, a clergyman, or a social worker.

- If you have a products liability case: ask an officer of a consumer organization or an insurance agent.
- If you have a discrimination case: ask an officer of a civil liberties or civil rights organization.

Lawyers' Advertisements

Listing a specialty in the Yellow Pages is considered a form of legal advertising, something that lawyers weren't allowed to do until 1977. Since then, legal advertising has become both widespread and more reliable, contributing significantly to the accessibility of the legal profession. The day has not yet arrived, however, when you can safely choose a lawyer merely on the basis of an advertisement.

The original reason that the American Bar Association banned advertising was to prevent incompetent or dishonest professionals from conning potential clients with misleading claims. Also, the whole idea of competing for clients seemed somehow beneath the dignity of the profession. "Many lawyers are opposed to legal advertising," says Stephen Gillers of the New York University Law School. "They say it will lead to *destructive competition*. Competition is all right, they say, for a business, where the goal is profits. But it is unseemly and demeaning for a profession where the goal is service to humanity. Lawyers who make this argument usually have many rich clients, and a lot of profits, and don't really need more."

It's true that, for the most part, the lawyers who have taken the most active advantage of legal advertising have been low-priced, marginal practitioners. These, unfortunately, are the very same lawyers who are most likely to deceive clients and render inadequate legal services. One attorney placed an ad in which he listed himself as "a former District Court judge." The claim was true, but the ad neglected to include certain embarrassing details—namely, that the attorney had been removed from the bench in 1967 for judicial misconduct that involved his assisting a housewife-prostitute avoid arrest.

But the mere fact that a lawyer advertises doesn't mean he isn't a good lawyer. Even F. Lee Bailey, the prominent criminal lawyer, and his partner Aaron J. Broder once placed an ad in several newspapers seeking "wrongful death and personal injury cases arising out of aircraft disasters."

The best way to approach legal advertising is the same way you should approach any advertising: skeptically. As an educated consumer, you should check out everything you see advertised before you buy the product. The same is true for lawyers who advertise their services. If an advertisement lists credentials, check them out independently. If it lists fees, make sure there are no hidden additional charges, and, if necessary, get assurances in writing.

Martindale-Hubbell *and Other Legal Directories*

There are several published directories devoted entirely to the legal profession. The most notable—and certainly the most substantial—is the seven-volume *Martindale-Hubbell Law Directory* (One Prospect Street, Summit, New Jersey 07901), which lists lawyers alphabetically first by location and then by firm. In addition to addresses and telephone numbers, the book gives other information about each lawyer, including date of birth, law school, academic honors, years in practice, position in firm, membership in professional associations and civic organizations, legal writings, professional awards and honors, and even lists of clients.

Each lawyer is also rated on the basis of confidential recommendations from other lawyers. Competency is rated *A* (excellent), *B* (good), and *C* (average). Reputation for honesty and integrity is rated *V* (very high) or not at all. This rating system may seem at first to be helpful, but, in fact, you should use it with considerable caution for the following reasons:

- A lawyer must be in practice for at least ten years to earn an *A* rating, five to get a *B* rating, and three to get a *C* rating, so excellent young lawyers go unrecognized.
- Because of the way they're compiled, the listings give some preference to lawyers associated with firms, especially large ones.
- High ratings often say more about how well a lawyer socializes in the legal community than about how well he practices law.
- By the time they reach the end of their careers, almost all lawyers get an *A-V* rating, making it an empty honor.
- Once a lawyer gets an *A-V* rating, the editors are loath to take it away. Some of the highest-rated lawyers may be past their primes.

Melvin Belli calls listings in *Martindale-Hubbell* the "worst criteria I know of." And Raoul Felder, the New York divorce attorney, says: "I know there are some lawyers for whose expertise I have no respect who have lovely biographies. On others, whom I do respect, there's only a line or two." In other words, you should use this directory not for its ratings but only as a source of additional information on lawyers who have been recommended in some other way. Besides, at $135 for the set, *Martindale-Hubbell* is too expensive for the average client, although copies are available at many libraries.

You needn't rely only on *Martindale-Hubbell*. There are several other legal directories that are also useful:

- *The Lawyer's Register by Specialties and Fields of Law* (5325 Naiman Parkway, Solon, Ohio 44139) has the unique advantage of being the only directory available that lists lawyers by specialty. Biographical information is given for some, but not all, of the lawyers listed and there is no rating system whatsoever.
- *The Lawyer to Lawyer Consultation Panel Directory* (5325 Naiman Parkway, Solon, Ohio 44139), available only to lawyers, lists only those practitioners who meet strict

standards of professional competence and integrity. The information in this directory is not completely inaccessible, however, because membership in the Lawyer to Lawyer Consultation Panel is noted in the more readily available *Lawyer's Register by Specialties and Fields of Law*, above.

- Directories are also published for various states and regions (Legal Directories Publishing Co., Inc., Suite 201, 1314 Westwood Boulevard, Los Angeles, California 90024). Because these directories are restricted to the lawyers in a single state or a single part of the country, they're much less costly than *Martindale-Hubbell*. So far, directories have been published for Alabama; Arkansas, Louisiana, and Mississippi; California (with sections on Arizona, Hawaii, and Nevada); Florida; Georgia; Illinois; Indiana; Iowa; Kansas; Kentucky; Minnesota, Nebraska, North and South Dakota; Missouri; the Mountain States (Colorado, Idaho, Montana, New Mexico, Utah, and Wyoming); New England (Connecticut, Maine, Massachusetts, New Hampshire, Rhode Island, and Vermont); New York; North Carolina; Ohio; Oklahoma; Oregon and Washington (with a section on Alaska); Pennsylvania; South Carolina; Tennessee; Texas; the Virginias, Maryland, Delaware, and the District of Columbia; and Wisconsin.

Like *Martindale-Hubbell*, these other guides are expensive, hard to find, hard to use, and not particularly helpful. Unless you can't find another source of recommendations, you should start your search elsewhere and use the directories only for checking the credentials of the lawyers already on your list of candidates.

The Yellow Pages

Some people find a lawyer by running their fingers through the "Lawyers" section of the Yellow Pages. There are a lot of bad ways to pick a lawyer, and this is surely one of the worst. All you have to go by is the sound of the name and the address. The address tells you something, of course. If convenient location is important to you, it can be helpful. But before you hire a lawyer, you should know a lot more about him than his address.

In a few cases a lawyer will list a specialty, but you should never take the listing at face value. A lawyer in Syracuse, New York, recently bought twenty-five listings in the Yellow Pages, each of them announcing his expertise in a different area of the law. Only three years out of law school, the lawyer was censured by the Appellate Division of the New York State Supreme Court for "overenthusiasm."

A FIRST STEP ONLY

As you have seen, there are many sources from which you can assemble a list of candidates. There is no *single* source, however, which you can go to for a simple, trustworthy recommendation. The best you can do is to use as many of the preferred sources as possible and cross-check the names each one yields. After that, it's up to you to arrange meetings with the lawyers you've selected and judge them for yourself.

5.
CHOOSING A LAWYER

Once you have assembled a list of candidates and cross-checked them with various sources, you should have narrowed the list to between three and five names. If you leave more than five names on the final list, you'll spend too much time interviewing.

The final step in the selection process is talking to each lawyer personally. This is the step that many people find the most difficult. They find the process of comparison shopping—especially when it involves lawyers—time-consuming, intimidating, and confusing. What do you want to know about each lawyer? What questions should you ask? What are the "right" answers? How should you make the final decision? This chapter is designed to make the difficult and often embarrassing task of choosing a lawyer easier and much more productive.

QUESTIONS TO ASK BEFORE THE INTERVIEW

There are a number of preliminary questions you should ask when you call to make an appointment with each of the lawyers on your list of candidates. These questions will save you the time and trouble of wasted interviewing:

• *"Do you handle my kind of problem?"* When you call for an appointment, always reconfirm that the lawyer does indeed handle the kind of legal work you need done. Otherwise, you'll just waste his time and yours.

• *"Can you handle a new client?"* If the lawyer does do the type of work you need done, but says he's busy, press the point. "Few lawyers in New York are so booked up that they can't take on another case," says Professor Stephen Gillers of New York University Law School. If the lawyer still refuses to see you, or refuses to see you within a reasonable period—say, about two weeks—give up and try another lawyer.

• *"Do you charge for initial meetings? If so, how much?"* You should ask whether the lawyer charges a fee for an initial interview—or consultation, as it's often called. Don't believe anyone who tells you to be suspicious of lawyers who don't charge for initial consultations. Many fine lawyers don't charge for first visits, as long as no substantive advice is sought or given.

• *"What is your typical fee arrangement in cases such as mine?"* You shouldn't eliminate a lawyer from your list of candidates simply because his fees are slightly higher than those charged by other lawyers you've interviewed. If they're substantially out of line, however, you probably should put him at the bottom of the list.

• *"Do you enter into lawyer-client contracts with your clients?"* Because lawyer-client contracts are still relatively rare, this may be a sticking point. If the lawyer is reluctant to enter into such a contract, we recommend that you consider another lawyer.

• *"What materials should I bring with me?"* Obviously, if you're to prepare adequately for the first meeting, you need to know if there are any special documents you should bring with you. On a first consultation, it's unlikely that the lawyer will want to see anything specific, but his willingness to handle your case may depend on certain facts which only documents can tell him.

ADVANCE PREPARATION

It's very important that you prepare for the initial meeting thoroughly. Preparation will give you the self-confidence you might otherwise lack. If you're being charged for the initial interview, it's especially important for you to do your homework because any wasted time during the meeting will cost you money. Besides, the better you prepare, the more likely it is that you'll make the right choice. Your advance preparation should include the steps listed below.

• *Assemble all necessary documents.* If you plan to talk about the specifics of your case with the lawyer, you should take any documents you consider relevant with you. If you plan to leave the documents with the lawyer, be sure to photocopy them in advance so you can continue to refer to them when necessary.

• *Write down everything you should mention.* Make notes covering how the problem began, how it evolved, and where it stands at present. You don't want to spend the lawyer's time and your money trying to remember all the details.

• *Make a list of questions to ask.* There are a lot of questions you should ask during the initial interview. The only way to make sure you don't forget any of them is to make a list beforehand and take it with you to the meeting.

THE INTERVIEW

The interview is the crucial stage in choosing a lawyer. It's your only chance to glean the kind of specific information you need to make an informed choice. Friends, relatives, other lawyers, and directories can all tell you something about a lawyer: his education, experience, and clients, for example. But they can't tell you what the lawyer is like. They can't tell you if he's supportive or arrogant, calm or harried, careful or contentious. Only a face-to-face encounter can answer *all* the questions you need to ask.

Don't Be Intimidated

The most persistent obstacle to effective, useful interviewing is a feeling of intimidation. Most people have a schizophrenic attitude toward lawyers and the legal profession: They tend to hold the profession in unjustifiably low esteem, but individual lawyers in unjustifiably high esteem—so high, in fact, that they are intimidated the minute they enter a lawyer's office. It's difficult, when you sit down to interview a lawyer, to remember that he's there to provide a *service*, just like a doctor, a housepainter, or a plumber.

The best way to overcome the feeling of intimidation is to understand it. If you're one of the many people who feel intimidated going into an interview with a lawyer—even when the lawyer's on your side—try to determine the source of the feeling. Among the most common sources of client intimidation:

• *The law is an impenetrable mystery*. It isn't the law that's impenetrable, only the jargon that lawyers surround it with. The lawyer is not a priest, he's just a professional with specialized training. If he can't explain the law to you in understandable terms, then he probably doesn't understand it himself.

• *All lawyers are intelligent*. Many lawyers are, in fact, exceptionally bright; some are not. Many are quick in some ways and slow in others. You want a lawyer who is smart, but don't hesitate to reject a lawyer who tries to make you feel intellectually inferior.

• *Lawyers deserve respect*. Many clients realize that lawyers enjoy a great deal of prestige, and they assume that their high social status demands deference. There is nothing inherently respectable about being a lawyer, so don't honor a candidate with your respect until it has been earned.

• *The subject of the consultation is difficult*. When you go to a lawyer, it's often in relation to a problem you're embarrassed to talk about. The difficulty of "confessing" to the lawyer only makes the situation more intimidating. You should remember that a lawyer is like a doctor: People's problems are his business. If he's a good lawyer, he should listen thoughtfully and show *no* signs of judgment or, especially, condemnation.

CRITERIA FOR EVALUATING A LAWYER

To take full advantage of the interview, you need to know what criteria to use in deciding whether a lawyer is right for you and what questions to ask to assess the lawyer's competence and compatibility.

We've listed some of those questions below. You shouldn't hesitate to ask any of them, or any other question you can think of. You should realize that some highly respected lawyers will consider some of them nosy or rude, at least at first, so you should tailor your own list of questions to the lawyer you're interviewing. Obviously, if you're interviewing the senior tax partner at a large corporate law firm, there's no need to ask him where he went to school or how well he did there. You can take it for granted that his academic performance was impressive. On the other hand, if you're interviewing a general practitioner in a very small firm, the question may be pertinent. Use your judgment. Even with the best lawyers, however, don't hesitate to ask the appropriate questions. At the very least, you'll put them on notice that you intend to be an alert and conscientious client. This first meeting will set the tone for the rest of your relationship.

If the lawyer refuses to answer your questions clearly and completely, press him a little. If he still refuses to answer, try another lawyer. "Don't let your lawyer be vague during the initial meeting," advises Professor Stephen Gillers. "Beware of lawyers who say '$500 now and then we'll see.'" You want to know as much as possible about a lawyer before hiring him; it's much easier not to hire a lawyer than to fire him after he's been hired.

TWELVE CRITERIA FOR EVALUATING A LAWYER

1. First Impression
2. Education
3. Experience
4. Reputation
5. Competence
6. Integrity and Confidentiality
7. Accessibility
8. Communication
9. Compatibility
10. Office and Staff
11. Need
12. Cost

First Impression

There are some things you can tell about a lawyer on first impression—long before the conversation settles down to substantive issues:

• *Promptness.* Does he make you wait around a long time before seeing you? A lawyer who sees you promptly is likely to handle your affairs promptly.

• *Energy level.* Does he have a high energy level? Law is hard work. If the lawyer looks tired or bored or both during the initial interview, you should be on your guard.

• *Articulateness.* Does the lawyer seem to ask the right questions? Does he get to the point quickly? If he fumbles in the dark when he asks about your problem, he may be in the same fix when he tries to solve it.

Education

A lawyer's education is one of the few objective measures of his ability. It's unfortunate that it's such an unreliable one. Most clients put far too much stock in where a lawyer went to school. This attitude is rooted in the history of a unified, elitist bar, and in the unusual quasi-aristocratic status of the legal profession. Whatever its roots, you should reject it.

Questions to Ask
- "Where did you go to law school?"
- "Were you a member of the law review or honor society?"
- "Have you taken professional education courses?"

"*Where did you go to law school?*" The law is a profession, not an academic discipline. But because law schools are extremely competitive, the fact that a lawyer went to a good law school suggests, at the very least, that he's reasonably intelligent. The fact that he went to one of the major schools—Chicago, Columbia, Harvard, Michigan, Stanford, or Yale, among others—is particularly impressive. Don't take it for granted, however, that a Harvard lawyer is a good lawyer. Harvard has graduated its share of incompetents.

In fact, you should probably think twice before hiring a graduate of a prestigious national law school to do your routine legal work. Lawyers who went to those schools (and concentrated on learning to "think like a lawyer" and second-guessing the Supreme Court) often get bored with routine work, work that doesn't involve much thinking. The problem is that *most* legal work is routine. Your divorce suit may proceed more smoothly if you're represented by a lawyer who studied divorce law, and who specializes in it by choice, rather than by a frustrated Archibald Cox who "majored" in constitutional law and who spends his afternoons daydreaming about an appearance before the Supreme Court.

Fancy law schools put fancy ideas in students' heads. Upon graduation, many of them aren't intellectually satisfied with a case unless it breaks new legal ground. If you don't care about breaking new legal ground, if all you want is a simple will, you're probably better off with a first-rate graduate of some less prestigious—but more practical—institution.

"Were you a member of the law review or honor society?" How well the lawyer did in law school is probably more important than the school's prestige. If you want to know how well he did but you feel awkward about asking his rank in class, ask him instead about his law school activities. At most schools, the best students from each class are appointed editors of the school law review; the top student is sometimes appointed editor-in-chief. A number of schools have established honor societies for their exceptional students. One, the Order of the Coif, operates on a national level.

"Have you taken professional education courses?" Perhaps even more important than a lawyer's law school education is his subsequent professional education. The law changes so quickly that most of what a lawyer learns in school is useless soon after graduation. To help lawyers keep up with recent developments, many state bar associations sponsor continuing education seminars for lawyers at every stage of their careers. Some—those in Iowa, Minnesota, and Wisconsin, for example—are making attendance compulsory.

Experience

A far more reliable index of a lawyer's ability than his education is his experience. So much of legal practice is rote detail and raw confidence that "hands-on" experience is by far the best teacher. In fact, until the twentieth century, most lawyers became lawyers by apprenticing in law offices, skipping the tedium and delay of law school altogether.

"How long have you practiced law?" Lawyers get their best training in the field, not the classroom. Law schools, says Supreme Court Chief Justice Warren Burger, "have done very well in preparing students in legal analysis and legal thinking," but haven't done well in preparing them for the courtroom.

Questions to Ask
- "How long have you practiced law?"
- "What do you consider your specialty or specialties?"
- "What experiences have you had outside private practice that might be useful in handling my case?"
- "Do you belong to any professional organizations?"

Only experience can do that. You should look for a lawyer who has completed his first three or four years of apprenticeship and is now an experienced professional in his own right.

"What do you consider your specialty or specialties?" If the lawyer does claim a specialty, you'll want to find out exactly what he means by "specialty." Be sure to ask what percentage of his cases are related to his specialty, whether he is certified by the state, whether he belongs to any professional organizations for fellow specialists, and whether he has received any special training in his area of specialization.

"What experiences have you had outside private practice that might be useful in handling my case?" Many lawyers begin private practice after spending some time in government service, and that experience can be very useful in private practice. There are well-worn paths, for example, from the Internal Revenue Service to the country's best tax law firms; from the United States Attorney's Office to the criminal bar; and from local real estate commissions to the local property law bar.

The experience doesn't have to be directly related to the practice of law in order to be helpful. For example, a lawyer who had experience as a marriage counselor might make a particularly good divorce lawyer. One who worked as a union official might make a good union lawyer. It's hard to believe that someone could practice skilled computer law without a background in computers.

There are also advantages to hiring a lawyer who has been

active in public affairs. An attorney who's been involved in local election campaigns, served on municipal boards and committees, or been elected to the boards of charitable foundations can smooth your way in the legal jungle. The politician he helped elect may be in a position to grant or deny your zoning application. The chairman of the charitable foundation may be the president of the bank from which you're requesting a loan. The legal system in the United States is one of the least corrupt in the entire world. But even here, the law regularly bends to the realities of personal politics.

"Do you belong to any professional organizations?" Active membership in local bar associations and other professional associations is sometimes a good thing, but not always. Often, it means that the lawyer is more interested in civic affairs than in the practice of law; more interested in socializing than in representing your legal interests effectively. "Unfortunately," says a Boston attorney, "the bar associations tend to attract only the brahmins and the social butterflies. The lawyers who are really into their work don't have time for it."

Reputation

There's a difference between a good lawyer and a lawyer with a "reputation." The first may simply do his work efficiently and effectively, with no fanfare. The second may or may not be an efficient, effective lawyer—he may just have a good press. Sidney Sachs, for example, is clearly the most talked-about divorce lawyer in Washington, D.C. Yet many Washington lawyers doubt the wisdom of his "put-up-your-dukes" approach to marital disputes.

In general, you should avoid lawyers with a high-profile reputation. They're usually more expensive and less accessible than their obscure brethren. You end up paying more money for less service—assuming, of course, that you can convince them to take your case in the first place. You would probably be better off with a less famous, less expensive, and less elusive attorney.

There's a major exception to this rule. If your case is particularly interesting, a famous lawyer may want to take it simply for interest's sake. The Edward Bennett Williamses and F. Lee Baileys of the world are partial to rich clients, but they're also partial to any client with a novel or controversial case. Unlike many lawyers, they're rich enough to enjoy the luxury of an intellectually challenging but nonremunerative case. Their interest is also aroused if the case will help maintain their high public profiles.

Questions to Ask
- "Has a state or local bar association ever disciplined you?"
- "Has anyone else ever brought a disciplinary action against you?"
- "Have you ever been sued for malpractice?"

"Has a state or local bar association ever disciplined you?" A disciplinary action is a serious blemish on a lawyer's record. In most cases, it will put him—and you—at a disadvantage with the judge and the opposing attorney. Such actions are particularly worrisome, needless to say, if they were brought for any wrongdoing directed at a client. If a lawyer "mingled" a client's funds with his own in the past, he may do it again.

"Has anyone else ever brought a disciplinary action against you?" Only a small percentage of complaints filed with local and state bar associations ever result in public disciplinary actions; lawyers find it distasteful to discipline one another. Therefore, you should try to find out if any such complaints have been filed but resolved prior to a determination by a grievance committee. Of course, a lawyer can simply choose not to tell you if there's been a complaint against him, and there's no record you can check to verify his denial. But you should ask this question anyway.

Because lawyers are so rarely disciplined, you should avoid

any lawyer who is given even a minor warning. Harold K. Bennett, an attorney in Asheville, North Carolina, quit the state's lawyer-discipline panel in disgust when a lawyer who had convinced a witness in a medical malpractice case to "give false testimony" (i.e., lie) was merely suspended for six months. It was, Bennett said, a "slap on the wrist. Such lenient treatment has a lot to do with lawyers' poor image. The public believes we sweep wrongdoing under the carpet."

"Have you ever been sued for malpractice?" A malpractice suit is the kiss of death for a lawyer's reputation. Because they are so rare and because they demand herculean determination on the part of the suing client, malpractice suits—even if they don't result in convictions—are indications that something was terribly wrong in a lawyer-client relationship. If the lawyer has been sued, chances are he'll want to explain the circumstances of the suit fully. You should listen, of course, and try to assess the significance of the incident. It's possible that he was merely the victim of a vengeful client. But unless the explanation is compelling, you should think twice about hiring him.

Competence

Too many lawyers are simply not competent. Chesterfield Smith, former President of the American Bar Association, has said that if he had a legal job to be done, he wouldn't trust one lawyer in five to do it right. What is competency and how can you evaluate it in the interview?

Questions to Ask
- "What is your definition of a competent lawyer?"
- "Do you enjoy your work?"

"What is your definition of a competent lawyer?" Most clients have no way to judge competence. If they're satisfied with the

way a lawyer handles their affairs, they think he's competent. But client satisfaction generally has less to do with true legal competence than with the lawyer's personal manner and his ability to work the client's will.

Although everybody has his own ideas about what constitutes a competent lawyer, there are some criteria about which there ought to be no disagreement. Here is a list of those "consensus criteria." When the lawyer you're interviewing tells you his idea of a competent lawyer, listen for these points:

- A competent lawyer researches legal problems thoroughly and efficiently.
- A competent lawyer applies the law wisely.
- A competent lawyer makes sound decisions.
- A competent lawyer anticipates problems that might arise and advises the client to avoid them.
- A competent lawyer handles problems promptly.
- A competent lawyer is able to draft legal documents that protect the client's interests and stand up in court.
- A competent lawyer attacks each new problem with vigor.
- A competent lawyer brings the client all satisfaction within the realm of possibility.

(For a more complete explanation of competence see Chapter 14.)

"Do you enjoy your work?" A lawyer who enjoys his work is apt to do good work. There are some lawyers who take so much pride in a job well done—or are so afraid of the consequences of a job poorly done—that they'll work indefatigably on something that doesn't yield an ounce of intrinsic satisfaction.

For every perfectionist, however, there is at least one corner-cutter: a lawyer who wants nothing more than to dispose quickly of the cases that bore him. The only pleasurable part of practicing law begins when he leaves the office and can enjoy the fruits of a profitable profession. Such lawyers are best avoided if you want conscientious and competent legal service.

Integrity and Confidentiality

In the eyes of the American public, Watergate dealt a deathblow to the integrity of the legal profession. Of course, the shyster-lawyer and the ambulance-chaser had always been part of our folklore: Lawyers have always had a bad press. But public distrust of the profession rose to new heights when John Mitchell, the former Attorney General of the United States, the nation's chief law enforcement officer, was led off to prison on charges of obstructing justice.

Most people are on their guard against outright dishonesty. But there are subtler, more common, and ultimately more destructive lapses in integrity which you should be aware of. Just as you don't want a lawyer who'll bill you for his afternoon coffee break, you don't want one who'll continue to handle your case when he knows he's in over his head and should be referring you to a specialist.

Questions to Ask
- "Who will have access to my files?"
- "How is confidentiality maintained?"

"Who will have access to my files?" You want a lawyer who will respect your right to privacy. He should be the only person with regular access to your files unless he specifically requests that someone else share that privilege. The only exception should be his secretary: A lawyer's secretary is his second set of eyes and you should expect that person to see everything the lawyer sees.

"How is confidentiality maintained?" A lawyer's ability to maintain the confidentiality of communications with his clients is extremely important. It's also an obligation under the Code of Professional Responsibility. But there's more to it than that. A lawyer's concern with confidentiality is a good indication of his

overall conscientiousness: the extent to which he takes the client's interests to heart. You don't want a lawyer who'll gossip about the possibly embarrassing details of your divorce case.

A lawyer's professional integrity can be measured by his attitude toward confidentiality. You should be able to tell from your conversation if he takes his duty of confidentiality seriously; if he doesn't, you should have serious doubts about hiring him.

Accessibility

No matter how good a lawyer is, he's of little use to you if he's not available when you need him. If he's constantly being pulled away from your case to handle someone else's affairs, he obviously can't give you the time and attention you need and deserve. So you should find out as much as possible about his schedule and his other commitments before hiring him.

Questions to Ask
- "How long should I expect to wait for an appointment?"
- "How will you divide the work on my case between yourself and a colleague?"

"How long should I expect to wait for an appointment?" You want a lawyer who is able to take your calls at any time—unless he's on another line or in conference—and to make appointments on only a few days' notice. Surprisingly, this is a factor that many people overlook in evaluating a lawyer.

In general, there are two things that directly affect a lawyer's accessibility. The most important is the volume of business he tries to handle. If he has too many clients, all of them will suffer because his time and attention are divided in too many ways. Ironically, some of this country's "best" lawyers (in the sense that they're highly respected and very well paid) are also some of its "worst" (in the sense that they're too busy with too many clients to give any of them the attention they deserve).

With any good lawyer, however, you can't expect him to see you at your convenience. Only if a matter is very urgent should you expect to see him the same day you call him for an appointment, but it should never take longer than four or five business days. No lawyer should be so busy that he has to put you off for weeks at a time.

"How will you divide the work on my case between yourself and a colleague?" If you develop a relationship with a lawyer, you should expect *him* to handle your problem. After all, you may have spent a great deal of time and energy finding him and checking his qualifications, and you know nothing about the people on his staff. Of course, if your problem is routine and a lawyer hands it over to a junior associate in order to save you money, you should be grateful. Just be sure that when the lawyer is handing your case over he has *your* interest at heart.

Communication

The ability to communicate—in writing or in person—is a crucial skill for a lawyer. If you're in the market for a litigator, this ability may be the most important quality to look for. Many cases that were lost on the law have been won on the lawyer's ability to communicate with the members of the jury. You don't really need to ask specific questions to evaluate the lawyer's communication skills. Every time he opens his mouth, he's either demonstrating or denying them.

A good lawyer should be able to communicate not only with judges and other lawyers, but with clients as well. The problem is that lawyers are trained to speak accurately and precisely, not clearly and concisely. Jerold S. Auerbach says, "The United States is a lawyers' paradise. So much of our institutional thought and language is legalistic that it is accepted without question. Legalese, aided and abetted by bureaucratic circumlocution, fills our vocabulary with what the Yale Law Professor, Fred Rodell, long ago labeled 'fuzzy-wuzzy words.'"

If you want to find out if the lawyer you're interviewing can communicate without the crutch of jargon, don't ask him directly if he uses it. Instead, ask him to explain the law that applies to your case—then listen for the jargon.

A lawyer's inability to communicate effectively can hurt a client's case. A New Hampshire woman complained: "My lawyer never once volunteered any information. I had to ask him on what grounds I was getting a divorce. I was unaware of the 'nonreconciliation of differences' type of divorce. It was a new law for New Hampshire at the time. I didn't want to lie about trumped-up grounds. When we finally got to court, the judge asked me to explain and I didn't know what to say. [The lawyer] didn't tell me I was going to have to talk. He just sat there and didn't say anything."

Compatibility

Even if a candidate has all the other qualifications, he may not be the right lawyer for you. A good lawyer-client relationship is like a good marriage: It requires trust and understanding. Is the lawyer flexible, willing to talk, sympathetic? Other client manuals pretentiously refer to this quality as "compassion." But to expect "compassion" from your lawyer when he draws up your will or incorporates your small business is just plain silly. It's really compatibility that you're looking for.

Questions to Ask
- "Are you and your clients satisfied with each other?"
- "Do you consider yourself adept at dealing with people?"

"Are you and your clients satisfied with each other?" It's difficult to measure the true value of lawyer-client compatibility. Fred

Grabowsky is an attorney in Washington, D.C., who specializes in complaints against lawyers. "Many lawyers," Grabowsky says, "need a better 'bedside manner.' They get the idea that a case is theirs, not the client's. It becomes an ego trip for the lawyer, and the client ends up as a bit player who doesn't know what's going on." It's certainly more pleasant to deal with an agreeable lawyer. And to the extent that a good working relationship contributes to good legal representation, by all means seek out a compatible lawyer.

Ask the lawyer if he is happy with his relationships with his clients. Note his reaction to the question. Is he hesitant or enthusiastic in his response? Does he respond warmly or coldly when he recounts experiences with clients? Is he confident of his clients' good feelings toward him?

You shouldn't place too much importance on the lawyer's bedside manner. After all, you shouldn't be going to a lawyer— or paying a lawyer's fees—if what you really want is someone to hold your hand. You're looking for an attorney, the ablest one you can find, not a friend. If you happen to get along and end up friends, consider that a dividend—not a requirement.

"Do you consider yourself adept at dealing with people?" In choosing a lawyer, you *should* consider how well he gets along with the people he deals with in handling your legal affairs. If, for example, the lawyer is negotiating a contract for you, it's important that he protect your interests, but it's also important that he do it without destroying your business relationships. Similarly, you don't want a divorce lawyer whose attitude will exacerbate the tensions between you and your spouse; a litigator who's afraid to hurt someone's feelings; or a criminal lawyer who will antagonize the judge or jury.

Office and Staff

If you've kept your eyes and ears open on your way into the lawyer's office, you've probably already got a good sense of the general atmosphere: whether the office runs efficiently, whether the staff operates effectively. But it doesn't hurt to ask the lawyer a few specific questions to assure yourself that he has the kind of support he needs to provide you with competent legal services at a reasonable price.

Questions to Ask
- "Does your firm have a good library?"
- "Is your firm computerized?"
- "How large is your support staff?"
- "Who else will be working on my case?"
- "Will the time of these other staff members be billed at lower rates?"

"Does your firm have a good library?" One of the primary advantages of a large law firm is its research facilities. Any law firm library should include the federal and state codes and cases, along with all the basic encyclopedias, treatises, directories, and other reference works. A more substantial library will also include research materials from other states.

"Is your firm computerized?" Even the smallest firm should have a word processor. Most incorporation papers, contracts, wills, and other routine documents follow standard forms. A word processor allows a firm to fill in the blanks with your information much more quickly, accurately, and cheaply than if a secretary had to type the documents from scratch. Firms also use computers for billing and data storage. The largest firms have access to Lexis, a computerized data bank including all the federal cases, and a growing number of state cases as well.

"How large is your support staff?" At the larger firms, most of the simpler work is probably handled by firm employees who are not lawyers: summer interns (law school students), paralegals (employees trained on the job), secretaries, librarians, and others. They generally have less expertise than an associate, but not always. An experienced legal secretary, for example, may

be much more knowledgeable than a new associate just out of law school. Because nonlawyers' time is billed at substantially lower rates, their services are often the best bargain in the law.

"Who else will be working on my case?" If the lawyer works in an office with three or more fellow lawyers, he may not do all your legal work himself. For reasons of efficiency and economy, he may handle the initial interview, see to the most difficult details, and supervise the progress of the case. Much of the work—perhaps most of it—may be undertaken by other lawyers in the firm. If, for example, your lawyer specializes in corporate law and you have a tax problem, he may send you on to the firm's tax partner. This shouldn't surprise or alarm you.

"Will the time of these other staff members be billed at lower rates?" If a particular problem requires long, hard, but relatively straightforward legal research, the lawyer may hand over that aspect of the case to a junior associate. He may do this even if it falls squarely within his area of expertise, simply because a junior associate's time is billed (or should be billed) at lower rates than a partner's time. If it's not, you're being overcharged.

Need

This is your first opportunity to talk about your case in detail and, more importantly, to get the lawyer's reaction. It's also your chance to get some free legal advice (assuming he isn't charging you for the initial appointment). You should listen carefully to his analysis of your case, your legal rights, your options, etc. Although based only on the sketchy information you provide, his insights will probably help you understand your case better, whether or not you hire him.

Questions to Ask
- "Do I need a lawyer?" ·
- "What steps will you take on my behalf?"
- "What do you think will be the results?"

"Do I need a lawyer?" You should always ask a lawyer whether you need legal assistance in the first place. Obviously, it's in a lawyer's interest to tell you that you do. If a lawyer tells you that you need representation even before you've fully stated the problem, be on your guard.

"What steps will you take on my behalf?" You should also ask the lawyer to tell you what he'll try to do for you. Here, too, the lawyer needs to strike a good balance. Since he's going on the basis of limited information at this point, he shouldn't appear too confident about the approach you should take. On the other hand, he shouldn't be too vague or evasive. A favorite device of some lawyers with new clients is to say something like "I know what to do" or "Just let me handle it." Don't be taken in.

"What do you think will be the results?" A lawyer should be able to lay out for you the general route—or routes—he thinks your case will follow. He should also be able to *guess* at the possible results, but that guess should be carefully hedged because he's basing it on a partial knowledge of the facts. Beware of any lawyer who "guarantees" results. The legal system is far too unpredictable for any lawyer, no matter how experienced, to speak with total confidence about the outcome of a case.

Cost

Of course, the final criterion you must use in selecting a lawyer is cost. Before you leave the initial interview, you should know how much the lawyer will charge you, what his billing procedures are, and any other information you need regarding payment.

Danger Signs

Sometimes a lawyer's failings are more obvious than his positive qualities. Here's a checklist of danger signs to look out for during your interview with the lawyer. You should remove his name from your list of candidates:

- when the lawyer puts off an appointment repeatedly;
- when the lawyer can see you any time, any day of the week;
- when the lawyer can't demonstrate that he's had the appropriate experience;
- when the lawyer doesn't seem interested in what you have to say;
- when the lawyer refuses to answer your questions to your satisfaction;
- when the lawyer makes you feel uncomfortable;
- when the lawyer guarantees the outcome of the case at the first meeting;
- when the lawyer attempts to limit his liability in your lawyer-client contract;
- when the lawyer is vague on the subject of fees;
- when the lawyer quotes fees that are significantly out of line with other fees you've heard mentioned.

MAKE SURE THE LAWYER KNOWS WHETHER HE'S HIRED

At the end of the interview, make sure the lawyer knows whether you're hiring him or not. If the answer is left vague, the lawyer may simply assume that you want him to begin work on your case immediately. If some other lawyer you interview makes the same assumption, you may end up in a very awkward situation—and you may not even realize it until you receive two bills in the mail. The best way to avoid any confusion is to make it clear at the beginning of the interview that it's merely an exploratory session and then, at the end of the interview, to tell the lawyer that you wish to think matters over.

THE LAWYER-CLIENT CONTRACT

The best way to avoid difficulties in any business relationship is to draw up a contract at the outset which anticipates all the problems that could possibly occur. Any good lawyer will tell you that—except when the business relationship is between you and him.

A lawyer-client contract does not have to be a formal document. A simple letter of agreement will suffice. But it should contain all of the important elements of the relationship:

- a description of the services to be rendered;
- the schedule according to which they're to be rendered;
- the fees and other charges;
- the billing procedure for the services.

The logical thing would be to have the lawyer draw up the contract or letter of agreement. If you do leave this up to him, however, be sure to review it carefully. Remember, this is one time when his interests and yours will not coincide.

Elements of a Lawyer-Client Contract

Your lawyer-client contract should include agreements on any subject that you think *might* become a point of contention. Each of your lawyer's obligations to you should be itemized, as should your obligations to him. For example, the lawyer should agree to bill you according to the fee agreement you've worked out *and* you should agree to pay him according to the same agreement (see Chapter 6, Fee Bargaining). And don't forget to put in a provision that specifies your lawyer's duty to cooperate, and your duty to pay, if you should decide to change lawyers before the case is completed (see Chapter 12, Discharging Your Lawyer).

A Sample Contract

In general, the contract should be tailored to the specifics of your relationship with the lawyer. Nevertheless, many of the same points appear in most lawyer-client contracts. The National Resource Center for Consumers of Legal Services, a public interest organization based in Washington, D.C., drew up the following sample lawyer-client contract for *Consumer Reports:*

- This agreement is entered into by and between ————— ("Attorney") and ————— ("Client").
- Attorney will perform the following services for Client: (Here specify the services to be performed.)
- Attorney estimates that legal services required by Client will take approximately ————— to ————— hours and cost between ————— and ————— as follows: (Here the lawyer lists hours and costs for handling different aspects of the case should certain variables occur.)
- Disbursement costs (filing fees, deposition and transcript costs, transportation, etc.) will be paid by Client. Attorney estimates that disbursement costs will be as follows: (Here the lawyer itemizes possible disbursement costs.)
- Prior to undertaking work beyond that initially specified, Attorney will provide Client with a written estimate of the additional time, fees, and disbursements involved and receive written permission from Client to undertake the work.
- Attorney agrees to explain the laws pertinent to Client's problem, the available courses of action, and the attendant risks.
- Attorney agrees to notify Client promptly of any significant development and consult with Client in advance on any significant decisions.
- Attorney agrees to send Client copy of all pertinent writ-

ten materials sent or received by Attorney pertaining to Client's case. Client agrees to reimburse Attorney out-of-pocket costs for the reproduction of those materials.

OR:

- Attorney agrees to make available to Client for reading in Attorney's office all written materials sent or received by Attorney pertaining to Client's case. At Client's request, Attorney will provide copy of any material to Client at Attorney's out-of-pocket costs.
- Attorney agrees to make all reasonable efforts to answer Client's inquiries promptly.
- Client agrees to pay Attorney as follows: (Here describe agreed upon fee arrangement.)
- Client may terminate this agreement, with or without cause, upon written notice to Attorney. Attorney shall return Client's file immediately upon Client's terminating this agreement. Termination shall not affect Client's responsibility to pay for legal services rendered up to the date of termination. Attorney may terminate this agreement for reasons permitted under the ———— (state) Code of Professional Responsibility.
- Nothing herein contained shall be interpreted to limit or restrict the Attorney's professional obligations under ———— (state) Bar's codes or canons.

_____

Attorney

_____

Client

Special Provisions. This sample lawyer-client contract includes most of the provisions required by the typical lawyer and client. If you want any additional provisions, negotiate them with your lawyer and ask that they be included as well. For example, if you don't want the lawyer to delegate any of your work to his subordinates, you'd better specify that in the agreement.

BEFORE MAKING IT FINAL: A CHECKLIST

Here's a summary of the issues to consider and reconsider before making the final choice of an attorney to represent your legal interests.

• *Ask the lawyer if his services are needed.* Another way to do this is to ask if there is some other, nonlegal way to resolve the problem. Otherwise, he might assume (although he shouldn't) that legal action is the only course you wish to consider. Ask him *why* a lawyer is needed.

• *Ask the lawyer to list the alternatives.* Also ask him to explain the advantages and disadvantages of each. This will put him on notice that you expect to be informed about the various alternatives at each step in the case and that you want to play an active role in choosing among them.

• *Ask the lawyer what he'll do for you.* What steps will be required to bring the case to a successful conclusion? If he refuses to go beyond vague statements about doing "whatever is necessary," or if he tries to plan the future in detail, try another name on your list of candidates.

• *Ask the lawyer how much of the work he'll do himself.* How much will he leave to junior associates, legal interns, paralegals, secretaries, or clerks? The lawyer should shoulder all the critical tasks himself. Less expensive personnel can perform less critical tasks so that costs can be kept down.

• *Ask the lawyer how long the work will take.* Better yet, ask him how long each step in the work will take. This will give both of you at least the start of a schedule for him to maintain and you to monitor.

• *Ask the lawyer about money.* Last but not least.

6.
FEE BARGAINING

Most people would no more bargain with their lawyer over fees than they'd haggle with the cashier at a grocery store over the price of a loaf of bread. They might complain to friends about highway robbery and the high cost of justice—just as they complain about gasoline prices. But they think both are really beyond their control. High legal costs, the assumption goes, are just a part of life, like death and taxes—in fact, very much like death and taxes.

Most lawyers, of course, are anxious to maintain the fiction that fees are set in heaven and therefore beyond the power of mortal men to change. The truth, however, is very different. Not since the days of minimum fee schedules have there been *any* limits on how little or how much a lawyer can charge for his services. As soon as you hear the words "going rate" or "standard fee," you should be on your guard. There haven't been going rates and standard fees since 1975, and the lawyer who tries to tell you they still exist is obviously putting his interest in making money above your interest in getting good, reasonably priced legal service.

Clearly, if there are no standard fees, then you'll have to negotiate them. You should consider that a privilege; there are not many consumer goods that you can still bargain over. Yet many people find the prospect of haggling over fees intimidating or distasteful, or both. If you're one of these, we suggest that you find somebody to do your legal shopping for you—or resign yourself to the probability that you will end up paying more than you should for legal services. If you're willing to try, we can give you a number of pointers and guidelines for getting the best lawyer at the best price. Remember: *Always* negotiate legal fees. If a lawyer will not negotiate, find another lawyer.

THE DIFFERENCE NEGOTIATING CAN MAKE

If you harbor any doubts about the importance of negotiating fees, consider the case of a wealthy Massachusetts widow who asked her late husband's attorney to be the executor of her husband's estate. Unfamiliar with business matters, she asked him in passing how much he would charge. He told her the fee would be 10 percent of the estate's value of $800,000, or $80,000. Enraged, she consulted other attorneys who offered to act as executor for as little as a $1,000 flat fee. She returned to her husband's attorney armed with the other prices and bargained him down to 1 percent of the estate's value, or $8,000. Of course, if she'd negotiated firmly, she probably could have gotten him to render the necessary service for even less. Still, she saved herself $72,000 simply because she was willing to face a lawyer and bargain.

Her case is a dramatic one, but it's not unusual. You can save yourself hundreds or even thousands of dollars in legal fees every time you see a lawyer if you're willing to ignore the embarrassment and negotiate firmly. Just keep two things in mind. First, there are no set prices for legal services. (Later, we'll give you some fee guidelines: *typical* prices for particular services. But even these are misleading. In some cases, a lawyer will lower a fee far below the typical range because your case has some special feature or because he sympathizes with your circumstances. There are even occasions when a lawyer will take a case for free.)

Second, remember that the market for legal services is now a *buyer's* market. That means that there are now many more people offering the service than there are people who want to buy it. In other words, there are a lot of hungry lawyers out there, anxious to find clients, and willing to work for substantially reduced fees. When you negotiate, keep in mind that for every lawyer who rejects your request for a reduced fee, there are three or four more who'll accept it.

WILL BARGAINING HURT YOUR CASE?

Many people wonder if haggling over fees will make it harder for their lawyers to serve them conscientiously and well. Is this a legitimate concern?

There's an old story about a barrister in England who tied a little pouch to the back of his gown so his clients could drop their payments in it without him seeing them. That way he could resist the natural tendency to argue more forcefully or work harder for those who paid him better. Unfortunately, that system hasn't become common practice (although barristers' gowns still have such pockets). Most lawyers care more about their fees than the charitable Englishman. Besides, if some modern lawyers tried the same trick, they might find their pouches empty at the end of the day.

There *is* a conflict between the "fiduciary" obligations of a lawyer and the commercial imperatives of his law practice. Therefore you shouldn't go into a relationship with a lawyer *expecting* to make it into a fast friendship. That's not to say that a friendship can't or shouldn't develop if you stay with one lawyer over several years.

So there are two things to keep in mind when you begin bargaining:

• *Don't bargain for the hell of it.* You are trying to prevent being overcharged for the services you need, not to see how little you can pay. The lawyer needs and deserves an adequate fee for his work and if you insist on less, you might be insulting him professionally as well as jeopardizing the quality of services he renders. Don't take unfair advantage, for example, of a young lawyer who is looking to build a clientele. He should be willing to work for less than the typical range, but he still deserves adequate compensation for his training and expertise. If you try to pay less, both the lawyer and you will be the losers.

• *Keep your eye on the goal.* Remember, the goal is *not* simply to find the lowest price, it's to find the best lawyer at the lowest price. Don't get so carried away in the search for savings that you lose track of the need for competent legal services. A bad lawyer is never cheap; in the long run, he can cost you hundreds or thousands of times his fee.

SHOPPING AROUND FOR THE BEST PRICE

As soon as you start shopping around for the best price on legal services, you'll be amazed at the range of prices you find. In a recent telephone survey of the Boston metropolitan area, the same divorce case, as described over the phone, drew fee estimates from $50 to $1,500. Just open any big city newspaper and you'll see advertisements trumpeting bargains on wills, adoptions, incorporations, and bankruptcies as well as the ever-popular uncontested divorce. Of course, what you never see in the papers are the prices being charged at the top of the line by old, well-established firms: They wouldn't dream of advertising their astronomical rates.

Ironically, this model of modern free enterprise was, for many years, a tightly run monopoly with carefully regulated prices and strict enforcement. Beginning in the 1920s, the local and state bar associations began to issue "minimum fee schedules" which stated, very flatly, what lawyers should charge for particular services. The lawyer could—and did—charge *more* if he wanted to, but he was prohibited from charging less. Thus, if you went to a lawyer and he quoted you a particular price for drawing up a will, it wouldn't do you any good to go to another one. His price would be the same—or higher. The bar associations claimed that this prevented price abuses by incompetent lawyers, thereby protecting the public and preserving the dignity of the profession. In fact, it encouraged artificially high prices, thereby bilking the public and lining the pockets of the profession.

All that changed in 1975, when the nine lawyers of the Supreme Court, in the remarkably unbiased (if overdue) *Goldfarb* decision, ruled that minimum fee schedules constituted price fixing in restraint of trade and were therefore a violation of the antitrust laws. The bar associations, of course, threw up their hands in anguish, bewailing the coming loss of professional dignity—and, no doubt, the coming loss of revenues.

The loss did come. Up to the time of the Supreme Court decision, the bulk of legal revenues had come from services that were cheap to provide but were billed at high rates: such routine tasks as writing wills and filing court papers. The fact that these services cost so little to provide meant that inexperienced lawyers could charge considerably less than the going rate and still make a profit. And that's exactly what they did. The result is that in most areas of the country, the prices of most legal services, especially the services most commonly performed, have been reduced by 30 to 60 percent from the days of the minimum fee schedules.

The Shopper's Guide

In one way, the bar associations were right to protest the removal of minimum fee schedules. The free market system does put an additional burden on the consumer. With so many different prices for so many different services, it can be a confusing job to find the lawyer and the price that are right for your particular problem. You do have to be careful and you can get cheated. But you could *always* get cheated—even under the old system. The difference is that if you get cheated now, chances are you'll pay less for it.

There's an old adage in the legal profession that you can tell a successful lawyer by his furniture. It might be more accurate to say that you can tell an *expensive* lawyer by his furniture. In fact, there are a number of factors that can help you determine, even before you begin negotiating fees, whether a particular lawyer is in your price range. When you're shopping around, keep these questions in mind:

- Does the lawyer offer a free consultation?
- Where is the lawyer's office located?
- Is the office run efficiently?
- Does the lawyer have a steady client flow?
- How old or experienced is the lawyer?
- Does the lawyer have income from other sources?
- Does the lawyer have a personal, professional, or political interest in your case?
- . Do you have any private connection with the lawyer?
- . Where do you live?
- . What was the lawyer's last job?

Does the lawyer offer a free consultation? An initial consultation, in which you tell the lawyer what your problem is and get some sense from him of how it should be handled, should be either free or relatively inexpensive. Many lawyers will charge nothing for initial consultations, even those whose rates are otherwise very high. Some lawyers will charge a nominal sum—$10, $20, or $30. Shop around for a freebie.

Where is the lawyer's office located? The primary expense in running a law office is overhead. All you have to do to know how much a lawyer spends on overhead is look around. Where is the office located? Is it in a high-rent building with an expansive (expensive) view? Is it in a high-rent part of town?

It's not true that all competent lawyers have fancy offices. Many don't consider a paneled office as important as providing good legal service at reasonable prices. Besides, do you really *want* a lawyer who cares more about his furniture or his view than he does about his clients?

Is the office run efficiently? This is a question you should start asking yourself as soon as you have any contact with the lawyer. Do you have to speak to two secretaries before you reach him or only one? Does he answer his messages promptly? When you go to the office, are people busy? Are there more secretaries than there are attorneys? The major part of overhead is personnel expenses. If you find a lawyer with a large staff, there are two dangers: One, he has to charge you more to pay all those people; and two, those people may end up doing the work that you're paying *him* to do.

Does the lawyer have a steady client flow? This is something you may have to ask the lawyer yourself. But it's important. If he has a steady flow of clients, he can spread his expenses—for secretaries, office rental, etc.—over a larger number of clients. A lawyer with only a few clients has to ask each of them to bear a larger share of the burden of keeping the office running. For the same reason, an office with several attorneys sharing the overhead and personnel costs is often more economical than a solo practice, and the lawyer can therefore charge lower fees.

How old or experienced is the lawyer? As a general rule, younger lawyers charge less than older lawyers. This is true not merely because of their age, but because they have less experience. This doesn't mean that you should always take a younger lawyer over an older one. There are times when the additional experience is worth the price differential. Especially if your case is not routine, a more experienced lawyer may actually save you money by dealing with the case more quickly than the younger lawyer. If the service you're seeking, however, is offered on a flat-fee basis, you're almost always better off to seek out a younger lawyer.

Does the lawyer have income from other sources? Again, this is something that you'll probably have to ask the lawyer directly. A lawyer with outside income is not as dependent on his income from legal fees and is therefore more likely to give you a price break. You should be aware, however, that it would be perfectly appropriate for a lawyer to refuse to answer this question.

Does the lawyer have a personal, professional, or political interest in your case? This factor will not often affect your shopping for a lawyer, but it's something you should be aware of. Lawyers are frequently fighting causes and using the courtroom or legal process as a weapon. Your case just might be of use as a weapon in these fights, especially if your dispute involves a political issue.

Do you have any private connection with the lawyer? This is the "my uncle is a lawyer" approach, which is often ridiculed but can be very useful. If you have family ties to a lawyer, you can probably expect a reduced fee. But you should also look around for school or church ties that you might be able to parlay into a fee reduction. There's no guarantee; it depends on whether the lawyer you find who attended your alma mater has warm memories or not. But any sort of connection is worth considering when you are negotiating a fee.

Where do you live? As a general rule, fees are lower in medium sized cities than in major metropolitan areas, and even lower in rural areas. As a city dweller, you may think that you're stuck with the higher fee levels where you live, but that's not always the case. If all you want is some routine service such as a will or an uncontested divorce, you are free to drive to a smaller nearby town and take advantage of the lower rates. Don't try this for complicated legal jobs, however, and don't venture across state lines, since the laws in the next state may not apply to your case.

What was the lawyer's last job? You should ask the lawyer what he's been doing recently. A lawyer who has just come off a protracted case may not have enough hold-over clients and may be willing to charge less in order to attract new clients who will take up the slack as quickly as possible. This is true in small firms and large firms alike, among both experienced and inexperienced lawyers.

None of these factors, you should note, has anything to do with the quality or competence of a lawyer. Yet they all affect the price of a lawyer. That should reassure anyone who thinks that the only good lawyer is an expensive lawyer.

Comparing Prices

After you've shopped around for several lawyers in your price range, you'll want to negotiate fee arrangements with each of them to see who can give you the best overall price. Just don't forget to get the *overall* price, not a partial price. When you ask many lawyers about their prices, they'll quote you their flat rate, or their hourly rate and an estimate of the time involved, but they won't give you any indication of other charges involved. The same is true of many legal clinics and law firms that advertise. They'll tell you that an uncontested divorce costs $150, but they won't tell you that there are additional court costs of $50.

So when you're shopping for prices, remember to figure into the cost of legal services the cost of additional (ancillary) services. Remember also that the lawyer should alert you to these fees and give you some idea how much they'll amount to in your case. If he doesn't, that's one strike against him. Here are the common sources of additional costs:

- investigative reports,
- medical reports,
- expert witness fees,
- nonexpert witness fees,
- filing and recording legal documents,
- service of legal process,
- subpoena fees,
- travel expenses,

- photocopying,
- deposition costs,
- printing charges.

The exact nature and extent of additional costs will depend on the nature of your case, but a reputable lawyer should be able to estimate them in advance.

BRASS TACKS: THE ART OF NEGOTIATING WITH YOUR LAWYER

In the previous section we talked about how to find a lawyer in your price range. If the service you need is routine, the lawyer may quote you an exact amount over the phone which compares favorably with the other quotes you've collected. So you sign a fee agreement with the lawyer and that's the end of fee negotiations.

But that's a procedure you should follow only in the simplest of cases: drafting a simple will, closing a routine house sale, filing papers in an uncontested divorce (in a no-fault state). If there are any complications at all, shopping will only help you select a lawyer who's in your *range*. You won't be able to get an exact price because the lawyer won't know yet how much work and time your business will require. It's in situations like this that you'll want to sit down and negotiate a fee agreement.

That doesn't mean you'll be able to get the lawyer to agree to an exact amount. A smart lawyer would never do that. He knows how often unexpected expenses are incurred if there's even the slightest complication. Linda Cawley of Cawley Schmidt & Sharrow in Baltimore recalls "a woman who came in and said she and her husband both wanted a divorce, so there wouldn't be any contest. I said, 'Fine, that will cost you $150.' Then she sort of laughed and said of course her husband only wanted to give her $75 a month and she thought she ought to have $100. I said, 'Lady, you've got a contest. That will cost you $350 plus $30 an hour for all my time over eight hours.'"

Although the rates that Linda Cawley quoted were reasonable, that was the time for the client to start negotiating.

Negotiating Techniques

So now you're in the lawyer's office and you want to negotiate a fee agreement. He quotes you a price which you think is too high. What can you say besides "I can't afford that" or "Won't you consider charging less?" What arguments can you use to get him to lower his fees? How do you respond to his arguments against a lowering them?

What follows is a basic course in how to argue fairly with a lawyer over fees. At all times you should observe good manners and good sense: Be pleasant, tell the truth, and be consistent in your arguments. Also:

• *Let the lawyer know that you've talked to other lawyers.* You should be sure to let the lawyer know that you're aware all lawyers don't charge the same prices. Let him know that you're a determined comparison shopper. This tells him two things: first, that he'll have to come up with a competitive price if he wants your business, and, second, that you're aware (or soon will be) of what is a reasonable price for the services you seek. The fact that you've made contact with other lawyers puts him on notice that you're a knowledgeable consumer. If you do hire him, that knowledge will help keep him "honest" throughout your relationship.

• *Remember that the lawyer would rather have a lower fee than none at all.* This may not always be true. There are some lawyers who have more than enough business; the loss of your case will not send them to the poorhouse. But in most instances, lawyers can always use more business. And if your case is relatively routine, they can take it on without incurring very much additional work. In other words, on most cases, a lawyer can turn a profit even if he discounts his fees by 50 percent. Use this knowledge to your advantage when negotiating. If your fee offer is reasonable, most lawyers won't let you walk out the door.

• *Don't believe it if the lawyer tells you he charges the 'going rate.'* As we said before, there are no such things as 'going rates' any more. There are prevalent rates and there are ranges of rates, but lawyers are no longer required to charge a specific minimum for a specific service as they were in the days of minimum fee schedules. If the lawyer insists that his charge is standard in the industry, you may have to remind him politely of the *Goldfarb* decision, which brought free enterprise back into the legal market.

• *Don't believe it if the lawyer tells you that anyone who charges less than he does is incompetent.* This is a common response if you mention that you have spoken to lawyers who will perform the needed services for less or if you suggest that comparison shopping will uncover better offers. There are a variety of factors which determine how expensive a particular lawyer's services are, and only a few of them relate to competence.

• *Assure the lawyer that his fees will remain confidential.* Many lawyers are reluctant to offer lower fees because they don't want it known that they charge less than the "high-rent" rates. They think it reflects badly on their firms if they offer "bargains" to particular customers. High fees, after all, are a sign of prestige. By assuring them that you won't divulge the fee arrangements, you might encourage them to consider lowering their standard, status-symbol rates.

• *Indicate more business in the future.* If there is even the shadow of a possibility that you'll have more legal business in the future (and who can confidently claim a future without legal problems?), you should inform the lawyer to that effect. Many lawyers will reduce their normal fees for a new client if there is a reliable indication that the client will be bringing them business over the years. Anything you can say to assure the lawyer that your relationship won't be just a "one-time" affair will make him more willing to lower his fees as a sort of introductory offer.

• *Don't hesitate to plead poverty.* Don't be afraid to tell the lawyer that you simply can't afford the fee he's quoted. If a

client is genuinely unable to pay, most lawyers will take that
into consideration. Many even feel a vague obligation to take a
few cases that are not remunerative, but are really a kind of
public service. The lawyer may see yours as one such case,
depending on what it's about. If you're a poor widow being
evicted by a merciless landlord, your chances of appealing to
his sense of justice are much better than if you're a merciless
landlord trying to evict a poor widow.

• *Offer to negotiate the terms of repayment.* This is not really a
way of getting a lower fee; it's a way of affording a higher one.
Many lawyers are willing to receive payment over a longer
period of time than is customary, and at a lower rate of interest
than banks charge on credit cards. Some refrain from charging
interest on time payments at all. There are dangers in this
approach, however: You may be tempted to say yes to a higher
fee than you can really afford to pay.

• *Point out any special circumstances in your case.* When negotiating with a lawyer, you should be quick to point out any details
that warrant giving your case special fee consideration. How do
you know if your case involves "special circumstances"? There
are two instances in which this might occur: if there is a moral,
philosophical, political, or social issue at stake, or if there is a
charitable or public service aspect to your case.

Most lawyers recognize that the cost of legal services is often
a barrier to dealing with important moral, philosophical,
political, or social issues. If you can convince them that
something they care about is at stake, they would be more
willing to reduce their fee. Besides, 90 percent of a lawyer's
usual business is boring. A case which involves an important,
challenging, or intellectually stimulating issue is water in the
desert to most lawyers. If your case involves a cause, take it to
several lawyers. One is bound to be sympathetic enough with
the case both to charge a lower fee and to pursue it more
vigorously.

Public service is good business for a lawyer. Many lawyers
harbor political aspirations; many more are simply civic-

minded. If an attorney thinks that he's serving the community by serving you, the fee is likely to be less important and his activities on your behalf are likely to be more spirited and rigorous.

• *Offer to barter for the lawyer's services.* Not everybody is in a position to trade a service for a service. But many lawyers are willing to discuss the possibility of alternate forms of payment. If, for example, you're a plumber, you have a valuable service which you can render to the lawyer in exchange for his services. If carried out properly, such an arrangement is not illegal, unethical, or even shady. So don't suggest it as if it were. It is merely "business for business" and it might make it possible for you to receive more and better legal service than you could otherwise afford.

• *Stress the routine, uncomplicated, uncontested nature of your case.* A lawyer is more likely to reduce his fee if it's clear that not much work is involved. "Work" in this sense can be equated with court appearances. The most routine lawyer's work (and therefore, theoretically at least, the cheapest) is the work that requires no court appearance, no filing of papers, just filling in the blanks. Among these are: real estate transfers, incorporations, drafting simple wills, leases, contracts, sales agreements, and similar kinds of "paper pushing." If your business involves these kinds of services, if there are no complications, and if no great sums of money are involved, you have a good argument for reduced fees. The next cheapest category of legal business is that which requires only a routine, perfunctory court appearance. Among these are uncontested divorces, adoptions, bankruptcies, and criminal cases in which there is either a guilty plea or an admission.

• *Suggest a multilevel fee.* If you argue that your case is going to be simple, routine, and uncomplicated, the lawyer might argue in response that something unexpected could come up that would require more work, more time, and therefore a higher fee. He wants to play it safe and quote a high fee. If this happens, suggest a "two-level" fee. If, in fact, nothing out of the ordinary happens and the case or business goes routinely, you pay the lower fee. If something comes up requiring more of the lawyer's time, you pay the higher fee. The same kind of arrangement can be worked out with the "sliding scale" fee discussed in Chapter 9. A word of caution, however: If you do agree on a multilevel fee, you should keep a careful watch on the lawyer's activities. You should also write into the fee agreement that he must notify you immediately if anything out of the ordinary comes up.

• *Don't hire the first attorney you contact.* There is a general tendency among American consumers to think that once they've discussed prices, they're obligated to buy. In bargaining for legal services, you need to resist that tendency. It may be especially difficult if the lawyer is giving you an initial consultation at no charge, but too much is at stake to stand on a misplaced sense of business etiquette. Some consumers think that if they even visit a lawyer's office they have to hire him. The whole point of shopping around is to compare both prices and individuals. You should seek out opportunities to meet lawyers face to face, and arrange as many initial consultations as time permits. The more lawyers you meet, the more sophisticated a consumer you'll become.

• *Demonstrate your knowledge of your case.* The best way to learn about your case is not to read law books, but to talk to as many lawyers as possible about it. Use the free, initial consultations as lessons. Take notes. Learning about your case will help you not only in the process of finding a good lawyer at a reasonable price, but also throughout the progress of the case and in your ongoing relationship with the lawyer you choose.

A Final Word on Negotiations

What do you do if a lawyer refuses to negotiate the fee, if he takes a "take it or leave it" attitude? Leave it.

THE FEE AGREEMENT: GET IT IN WRITING

After a full discussion of fee arrangements, get a fee agreement *in writing*. It is impossible to overemphasize the importance of this advice. A written agreement is the best form of insurance you can have against the kinds of disputes that inevitably arise when money is involved. The following is a case in point.

A Minnesota man was severely crippled in a railroad accident and sued for damages. He hired an attorney who agreed, according to the client, to handle his case for a contingency fee of 20 percent of the damages awarded. That was below the then-standard rate of 33⅓ percent, but the lawyer was young and inexperienced and, the client insisted, he had negotiated a lower percentage fee.

The client finally won and won big. He collected more than half a million dollars in damages and paid the lawyer 20 percent, or $100,000. The lawyer turned around and sued him, saying that he was entitled to the standard contingency award of one third and that he had never agreed to take less. The client had trouble finding another lawyer who would take his case against the first lawyer and ended up paying an additional $65,000 in fees.

Perhaps the lawyer had never agreed to take less and the client was just greedy, but only the client, the lawyer, and God know for sure what their agreement really was.

By putting the fee agreement in writing, you can avoid this kind of costly dispute. You can also clarify the terms of the agreement, increase your confidence in the lawyer and the lawyer's confidence in you, and prevent the kind of bickering and bad feelings that can undermine a good working relationship. The benefits are well worth the extra time it takes to put everything down on paper.

Having the fee agreement in writing is also in the lawyer's interest. If the agreement is only verbal, or if there is no explicit agreement at all, courts tend to favor clients in fee disputes. That isn't always the case, as the man from Minnesota can testify, but it's enough to encourage a lawyer to put the fee arrangements in writing. It's also a good reason to question a lawyer's refusal to do so.

What Should Go Into a Fee Agreement?

Here are the salient points that should be covered in a fee agreement:

- circumstances under which you must pay legal fees,
- manner in which the fees will be computed,
- manner of payment,
- form of the bill,
- lawyer's basic hourly rate,
- estimate of total hours required,
- manner in which a contingency fee (if any) is to be calculated,
- estimate of additional costs,
- amount of deposit or retainer,
- breakdown of all hour and cost estimates,
- total charges.

• *Circumstances under which you must pay legal fees.* This is the so-called "trigger" clause, meaning that it specifies what must happen before you pay. If, for example, you're selling real estate, you may arrange to pay the legal fees upon closing. If the lawyer is working on a contingent basis, the fee agreement should specify that he's to be paid only when and if you receive money either in the form of a settlement or in the form of court-awarded money damages.

• *Manner in which the fees will be computed.* If, as in the case of the house sale, the fees are to be a percentage of the sale price, you should include that percentage in the fee agreement. If fees are to be determined on an hourly basis, that should be specified. It's common for total fees to consist of a combination of percentages, hourly billings, and ancillary costs. The rate for each and an estimate of total charges should be included in the agreement.

• *Manner of payment.* Will the lawyer bill you monthly, semiannually—or just periodically, when the spirit moves him? There is no established norm in the profession, so you should specify it in the agreement. Also specify what form the payments will take: check or cash.

• *Form of the bill.* The fee agreement is the place to specify what the bill should include (see, Chapter 7, Calculating the Bill).

• *Lawyer's basic hourly rate.* This should be the result of the negotiation process. The rate may vary, depending on what it is the lawyer is doing for you. For example, he'll probably ask for a different hourly rate for court appearances than for client conferences. All these should be specified. Some lawyers offer an exemption: a certain number of hours for which they won't charge. Only when the total time exceeds the exemption will the hourly rate go into effect. That exemption (often eight hours) should also be specified.

• *Estimate of total hours required.* Depending on the nature of the case, this may be a "hard" or reliable figure, or it may be just a "soft" guess. The lawyer may want to protect himself by including different time estimates depending on what happens to the case. For example, twenty hours if the case is settled prior to trial, fifty hours if it goes to trial. Normally, this is an acceptable procedure.

• *Manner in which a contingency fee (if any) is to be calculated.* Obviously, this should only be included in the agreement if you've arranged for the lawyer to handle your case on a contingent basis. It's crucial that the agreement contain the exact percentage figure and the deductions from the total award which should be taken *before* the lawyer's share is figured. (See Chapter 9, Negotiating a Contingency Fee.) In other words, if there is a $100,000 award and the lawyer is entitled to 25 percent under the terms of the agreement, and if there have been $20,000 in expenses, the lawyer should get $20,000 (25 percent of $80,000), *not* $25,000 (25 percent of $100,000).

• *Estimate of additional costs.* A good lawyer should be able to estimate in advance the various ancillary costs that will arise. Again, he may want to give two estimates: one if the case is settled, one if it goes to trial. But these estimates are important because they give you a sense of what the *total* cost will be, not just the cost of the lawyer's services.

• *Amount of deposit or retainer.* In some cases, especially cases taken on a contingent basis, the lawyer will ask you to put up a relatively small sum of money at the start to cover his expenses. If the lawyer is reasonably prosperous, or if you are unable to afford the retainer, the lawyer should waive it. Make sure the waiver is stated explicitly in the agreement. If you do pay him a retainer or put down a deposit, record the amount in the agreement and also get a receipt.

• *Breakdown of all hour and cost estimates.* It's not sufficient if a lawyer tells you simply what his hourly rate is and how many hours the task will take. You should also ask for a breakdown of the hours required according to the individual tasks that need to be performed, and, even more important, according to *who* will be performing those tasks. For example, filing an uncontested divorce might take six hours, but some of that work, including filling out some standard forms, doesn't have to be done by the lawyer himself—in fact, *should* be done by a secretary or paralegal. By insisting on a breakdown of charges, you guard against being charged lawyer's wages for secretarial work.

• *Total charges.* The lawyer should be willing to give you an estimate of the total cost of providing the needed services. Again, he may want to hedge his bets by specifying a different estimate for several different circumstances, but if he has prepared the estimates carefully, they'll give you an accurate idea of what you can expect to pay.

Before You Sign

You should never sign any agreement until you're satisfied (not necessarily happy) with all of its provisions. This is especially true of a fee agreement with a lawyer. As we've said before, there is an inherent conflict between the lawyer's role as counselor and the lawyer's role as businessman; nowhere is this conflict more of a problem that in drawing up fee agreements.

If you have any doubts about whether or not you should sign, take the draft agreement home and think about it; show it to friends or business associates. You may even want to consult another lawyer, although doing so can be awkward and will probably cost you money since you won't be offering the attorney you consult any immediate prospect of employment.

Once you do sign, make sure you have a copy of the agreement that is signed by you and by the lawyer. Take it home and keep it in a safe place.

What Happens to the Fee Agreement If the Lawyer Withdraws?

What becomes of the fee arrangements contained in the agreement if the lawyer withdraws from your case before finishing the services specified in the agreement? The answer to that question is complicated, but in general it hinges on the *cause* of the lawyer's withdrawal.

If the lawyer withdraws because the client is guilty of misconduct (illegal activities, perjury), the client is normally obligated to pay the bill in full. If, on the other hand, the client discharges the lawyer because of the *lawyer's* misconduct, there's usually no fee obligation. Finally, if the lawyer withdraws at the client's request simply because the client wants a change of attorney, the client is usually obligated to pay the lawyer for the work he's done up to the time of withdrawal. If the agreement sets a flat fee, the amount is usually determined on a pro rata basis. The same solution is used if the lawyer withdraws because of illness or other incapacity. (See Chapter 12, Discharging Your Lawyer.)

It's Never Too Late

It's never too late for a fee agreement. If you already have a lawyer, but don't have an agreement, start talking about one. If you hire a lawyer before a fee agreement is worked out, don't be too concerned. If a dispute arises, a fee agreement arranged after a relationship between lawyer and client has already been established is usually construed against the attorney. The theory is that, once the client begins to rely on the lawyer, the lawyer has an unfair bargaining advantage.

7.

CALCULATING THE BILL: GENTLEMANLY TRADITION OR CONSUMER RIP-OFF ?

A major corporation paid a Wall Street law firm millions of dollars every year to defend it in a long-term antitrust suit which the government eventually dropped. A young associate at the firm assigned to that suit reported that some colleagues were billing the corporation for time spent playing softball and tennis on the firm teams. One lawyer on the case logged an astonishing 3,500 hours in one year on the corporation's dole. When asked about these abuses, a corporation spokesman responded, "We wouldn't know because we don't get a bill broken down by hours . . . We have a very long and very interesting relationship" with our law firm.

Despite the difference in scale, this kind of "interesting relationship" is typical of most lawyer-client relationships today. The unspoken rule in such relationships is that the client doesn't ask any questions about billing and the lawyer doesn't answer any. This neat arrangement is partly a matter of courtesy and discretion: The lawyer-client relationship is supposed to be built on trust, not dollars. To talk money is somehow to taint that trust. But the arrangement is also a matter of convenience. If the lawyer doesn't have to justify his charges to the client, he doesn't have to expend the time or effort to keep track of those charges. He also doesn't have to understand or even think about the economics of practicing law. Ignorance is, indeed, bliss.

IN THE DARK: WHAT CLIENTS DON'T KNOW ABOUT LEGAL BILLING

There is, of course, a less flattering interpretation of the typical lawyer-client relationship. "The secret of getting along with a client," says a San Francisco lawyer in a small but well-known firm, "is to keep them in the dark. The less they know, the better I like it—and the better *they* like it. That's especially true when it comes to fees. Less said the better." In the dark is exactly where most clients find themselves when it comes to calculating fees and billing procedures.

Although there have been some changes in the billing procedures of major law firms—sparked mainly by increasing criticism from clients about rising legal expenses and greater cost-consciousness—many are still billing the way they have for years. Every month or two, the client gets a letter on handsome engraved stationery that says little more than: "Matter of A versus B: $25,000."

Why do lawyers keep their clients in the dark about what they're doing on the clients' behalf? They say it's because so much of what they do is done while the clients are not around. Sometimes that's true. But sometimes lawyers keep their clients in the dark about what they're doing because they're not doing very much. And if the clients *know* they're not doing very much, they might begin to question what the lawyers *claim* they're doing on the bill. "They don't exactly lie, but my partners keep utterly inadequate records," admits one Washington attorney. "They may shoot the breeze with other partners for an hour, but forget later and mark it down as client time."

For the Record: Where the Time Goes

Procedures for keeping track of time spent vary from one firm to another. Sometimes they even vary from one lawyer to another *within* a firm (although most big firms have set policies). Some lawyers maintain formal records, while others merely estimate the time they've spent working for a particular client. That process of recollection and estimation usually takes place only once a week, sometimes only once a month. Can you imagine trying to figure out, at the end of the month, how much time you've spent, say, reading magazines, grocery shopping, writing letters, or arguing with your spouse?

The rising chorus of criticism has finally caught the attention of some lawyers. The result, says Houston attorney Kraft Eidman, is that many are becoming more conscious of costs and procedures. "I think lawyers are more aware of costs than they were three years ago," Eidman claims, recalling the not-so-distant days when lawyers didn't even bother keeping records. At his firm, Fulbright & Jaworski, all the lawyers are now working for "Big Henry," the computer that keeps track of lawyers' time and billing. Eidman laments: "It's taken a lot of fun out of practicing law."

"Calculating" Legal Fees

Why does a young associate in a medium-sized firm charge $50 to $70 per hour? Does that figure represent a careful calculation of the cost of providing that hour's worth of service plus a fair profit? Hardly. As in every aspect of fee setting and billing procedure, the only thing the "standards" have in common is their arbitrariness. Lionel Kestenbaum, a lawyer with the Washington firm of Bergson, Borkland, Margolis & Adler, admits that legal fees are often calculated on a "seat-of-the-pants" basis.

In the old days, of course, when practicing law was more "fun," calculating fees was easy. All a lawyer had to do was consult the minimum fee schedule. Even today—despite the occasional inroads of legal clinics and lawyers who advertise—it's remarkable (and a little disturbing) how consistent the prices for similar services are among most small law firms in the same area. It's not entirely clear whether lawyers still use the fee schedules informally, or whether no one has bothered to rethink the price list since it was formally abolished.

If you want a rough rule of thumb, here's one that works with most medium-sized, reputable firms. A lawyer's time is generally billed at hourly rates equal to twice his annual salary divided by 1,000. Thus, a lawyer who earns $40,000 a year (just out of law school if he's in New York) is billed at $80 an hour. Obviously, that's not the way the hourly rate *or* the salary was calculated in the first place; it's just a way of imposing some rhyme and reason on the otherwise crazy quilt of legal fees.

HOW YOUR LEGAL BILL SHOULD BE CALCULATED

There are a variety of ways of calculating legal fees and no one of them is right for all occasions. Each one has different advantages and disadvantages which make it better suited to some kinds of cases than to others. Unfortunately, you can't always rely on the lawyer to tell you which one is most economical in a given situation. For example, no lawyer will take on a contested divorce for a flat fee because he has no way of knowing how long the case will take. Most lawyers, however, won't bother telling you that you might save money by paying them to pursue a personal injury claim on an hourly basis. Why? Because—if the claim is a good one—they know they can make more money by pursuing it on a contingent basis.

As we've seen before, whenever the question of money comes up, the conflict between the lawyer's interest in running a profitable business and his obligation to you as a client is at its most acute. If you don't want to rely solely on his advice, you should enter fee discussions armed with as much knowledge as possible.

Remember, there's nothing "legal" about legal fees. You don't have to be a lawyer to understand them, or to bargain over them. When it comes to payment, a lawyer is no different from a plumber; you should scrutinize fee arrangements with the former as closely and confidently as you would fee arrangements with the latter. To help you do this better, you should learn about the different types of fee arrangements: their rationales, their advantages and disadvantages, and the types of cases for which each is appropriate.

Hourly Rates

Most legal fees are figured on an hourly basis. In fact, the hourly rate is so routinely used that some lawyers are beginning to wonder if it isn't overused. Patrick Higginbothom, a federal judge from Dallas, accuses lawyers of being "mesmerized" by hourly charges. "We ought to at least acknowledge," he says, "that it is questionable whether the hourly fee arrangement gives incentives to cut costs."

The judge knows what he's talking about. The hourly fee is, for reasons we've already discussed, an invitation to abuse. That abuse can take the rare form of consciously nefarious practices—the Chicago lawyer who charged his clients for twenty-three hours out of every twenty-four-hour day; or it can take a much more common and "innocent" form—the Wall Street associates who pad their diaries by charging for bathroom time.

There are occasions, however, when there's no reasonable alternative to hourly charges. When they are essential, the best way to prevent abuse is to monitor your lawyer's activity closely by using the monthly bill as your guide.

Hourly Fees
Advantages
- You pay only for work actually performed.
- You can cut costs by shopping for a lawyer with a low hourly fee.
- You can monitor the lawyer's level of activity more closely.

Disadvantages
- The total cost can't be determined in advance.
- The lawyer's estimate of the total time required is not always reliable.
- Charges can skyrocket if unexpected complications arise.
- Payment is usually due before the outcome of the litigation is known.
- Cost effectiveness depends on the qualifications of the particular lawyer.

Hourly rates range considerably from one lawyer to the next depending on the demands on the lawyer's time, the extent of his knowledge, and his record of success. At a legal clinic, you shouldn't have to pay more than $25 to $50 per hour for a lawyer's work. At a big law firm, the top partners may charge an hourly rate of $200 or more.

The fact that the range is so wide makes it possible for you to cut the costs of legal services by shopping around for a lawyer with a low hourly rate. But you should take some precautions: What looks like a bargain isn't always a bargain. When a lawyer plans to charge you for his work on an hourly rate, it's especially important that you inquire about his training, experience, and background *in your type of case or legal matter*. That training and experience can save a great deal of his time and, therefore, of your money. If your case is complicated or unusual, it might take an inexperienced lawyer with a low hourly rate three or four times as long to complete it than a lawyer who has handled similar cases and charges twice the hourly rate.

The major drawback to hourly fees is that they're open-ended. You don't know how much you'll eventually have to pay. The lawyer should give you an estimate of the total number of hours required, but often that estimate is based, of necessity, on faulty or incomplete information. Complications can arise which add hours or even days to the total. This is a special problem if you become involved in lengthy litigation, when an hourly fee agreement can result in a long series of monthly bills that must be paid long before the outcome of the litigation is known.

Hourly fees are usually appropriate for the following kinds of activities:

- drafting contracts,
- writing letters or making phone calls,
- negotiations,
- settlement conferences,
- trials.

Flat Fees

A lawyer will usually charge a flat fee when a service is relatively routine and he knows how long it will take. Most legal services you see advertised are offered for a flat fee: divorces $150, incorporation $100, wills $35. The lawyer can charge these low fees because he knows there won't be any complicating factors. If there's even a hint that your case will require the lawyer's personal attention, you'll be charged more, sometimes much more, probably on an hourly basis.

Flat Fees

Advantages

- You know in advance how much the charges will be.
- They can be paid in segments.
- Payment can be financed, allowing you to secure additional legal services.
- They permit cost savings if your case is routine.

Disadvantages

- They depend on a careful and accurate estimate of the time required.
- They may have to be renegotiated if complications arise.
- They have built-in disincentives.
- Spreading or financing payment can cause extra spending on legal services.

Flat fees are very inviting. When you see ads for "DIVORCES, ONLY $150" in the newspaper or on television, it's easy to assume that, no matter what your individual case may be, a divorce will cost you only $150. You may think your divorce is "uncontested," but you won't know for sure until the process is in motion. That's the primary problem with flat fees. If everything goes routinely—no complications, no contests, no disputes—then they can be great money savers. If, however, any sort of problem arises—and in most cases one does—they get thrown out the window and you have to renegotiate your fees all over again.

The primary advantage of flat fees—that they're set in advance—can also be their primary drawback. If, for example, a lawyer has agreed to do a certain job for you for a certain price, and then discovers that it will require more effort than he figured on, he may be tempted to cut corners and put in less work than is necessary to do a good job. The other possibility is that he'll come back to you and ask to renegotiate the flat fee because of the additional work required. Although there are occasions when unforeseen complications warrant renegotiating a flat fee, you should be a little leery of any such request and insist that it be fully justified in writing.

Finally, some lawyers will permit you to spread out payment of a flat fee over a much longer time than is required to perform the service. That can be a real convenience, but it can also be a trap. You could end up buying more legal services than you need and paying more than you can afford.

Flat fees are usually appropriate for the following kinds of activities:

- preparing a simple will,
- drafting a simple contract,
- filing an uncontested divorce,
- incorporating a small business.

NOTE: Although it isn't common practice, you might save a lot of money by trying to negotiate a flat fee instead of a percentage fee for house closings, negotiating other real estate transactions, executing estates, and probating wills. This is especially true if the property involved is particularly valuable.

Percentage Fees

When you ask a lawyer to help you transact some business with a specific asset or group of assets, and the value of those assets can be determined with some accuracy, his fee is often based on a percentage of that total value. The most common example is the sale of a house or other piece of real estate. It's common practice for a lawyer to take a percentage (usually about one percent) of the value of the house as his fee for the closing.

In most cases, percentage fees are a windfall for the lawyer and a bane on the client. This is especially true if the property is valuable: A lawyer often does the same amount of work whether the house is worth $50,000 or $500,000, but the difference in fees for the two jobs is substantial—$4,500. It's possible, however, to work out a sliding scale of percentages so that the higher the sale price, the lower the lawyer's percentage. (See Chapter 9, Negotiating a Contingency Fee.)

Despite the obvious drawbacks, percentage fees are often required by law. They do make certain legal services available to people who could not afford a lawyer's hourly fee.

Percentage Fees
Advantages
- They can be calculated in advance (at least as a percentage of value).
- Percentages can be negotiated.
- No fees are incurred in advance of the transaction.

Disadvantages
- Total amounts can be high if the assets involved are especially valuable.
- Percentages do not accurately reflect time spent on the transaction.
- They may not be negotiable if required by law.

The fundamental problem with percentage fees is that they bear no relationship to the services which the lawyer actually provides, or to the amount of time required to provide them. This can result in a variety of inequities. If the assets involved are valuable and no special work is required, the lawyer ends up overpaid. If the assets aren't particularly valuable and complications arise that require his attention, he may not be enthusiastic about spending the necessary time and effort because his share will be the same in any event. You should look askance at any method of paying a lawyer (or anybody else) that doesn't encourage him to protect your interests and reward him for good work.

Percentage fees are usually appropriate for the following kinds of activities:

- probating a will,
- acting as executor of an estate,

- acting as a court-appointed receiver,
- closing a house or other real estate transaction.

Contingency Fees

Contingency fees are a subject of controversy in the legal profession. A contingency fee is based on a percentage of whatever money the client ultimately receives from the suit. Because contingency fee agreements are negotiated at the beginning of a law suit, the lawyer doesn't know exactly what he'll be paid, and you, as a client, don't know exactly what you're giving away. Both are "contingent" on the money you eventually get. That money can come in the form of a settlement before your case goes to trial, or it can come after trial in the form of damages awarded by a judge or jury.

A couple of key points about the contingency fees ought to be obvious. First, a lawyer simply won't take a case on a contingency fee basis unless he thinks you have *some* chance of winning some money. So if you're suing for something other than money, you probably won't get a lawyer to take your case on a contingency basis unless there's a good possibility that the person you're suing will "settle," that is, give you money to drop the suit.

Second, it should be obvious that a contingency arrangement isn't always the best thing for the client. If someone offers you a large sum of money to drop your suit, you may still want to press ahead to trial. Your lawyer, on the other hand, may want to avoid the work involved in a trial and take his share of the settlement offer. This isn't just idle speculation. Contingency fees are notorious for the conflicts of interest they often spawn between lawyer and client.

Take, for example, the case of a prominent New York attorney who represented the son of a man killed in the 1977 collision of two jumbo jets in Tenerife, Canary Islands. When the attorney sued Pan American Airlines for $5 million on behalf of his client, Pan Am's attorneys didn't contest liability, but they offered to settle the son's case for $80,000. The attorney refused, but offered to settle instead for $275,000, which Pan Am refused in turn. The matter went to trial, and the jury decided that the son deserved nothing because he had not been close to his father and therefore had lost nothing by his death.

At that point, in order to avoid an appeal, Pan Am offered to settle for $25,000. The attorney accepted the offer this time, and took as his contingency fee $10,000, leaving the son with $15,000—instead of the $80,000 Pan Am had originally offered. The moral: When dealing with a contingency fee, a lawyer's enthusiasm can sometimes get you more money, but a lawyer's greed can sometimes get you in trouble.

The *theory* of contingency fees is that they make it possible for a client to pursue claims he couldn't afford to pursue if he had to pay the lawyer on an hourly basis. Also, by giving the lawyer a stake in the outcome, the arrangement encourages him to work harder on the client's behalf. In most cases, the practice vindicates the theory. But the potential for conflicts of interest and the opportunity for abuse place an extra burden of careful oversight on the client who chooses a contingency fee arrangement.

Contingency Fees
Advantages
- They encourage claims that might otherwise go unpressed.
- They require no money up front.
- They encourage the lawyer to work harder on the case.
- They can be negotiated.

Disadvantages
- There is considerable risk of conflicts of interest in dealing with settlement offers.
- The total costs can't be calculated.
- Lawyers hired on a contingency basis are harder to replace.

- The lawyer can receive a windfall.
- Contingency fees can't be used in all cases.
- The lawyer may require a retainer.

Conflicts of interest and percentage abuses are the primary disadvantages of the contingency fee arrangement. The latter are most common when the defendant in your suit doesn't dispute liability. If that's the case, your lawyer probably won't be required to do very much work. If he's working on a 33⅓ percent contingency basis and you're awarded a large sum of money, he can make out, literally, like a bandit.

You can guard against that kind of abuse in the fee agreement by providing for a multilevel fee in which the attorney's percentage of the award or settlement varies depending on whether the defendant disputes liability, whether the case goes to trial, and other relevant factors. (See Chapter 9, Negotiating a Contingency Fee.)

The conflicts of interest are much harder to guard against and much harder to detect once they do arise. If, for example, your lawyer determines that your claim doesn't have much value, he'll be tempted to stop working hard on it. Unless he chooses to tell you that his attitude about the case has changed, you might find it hard to detect the slackening of his enthusiasm. Or, he might start pursuing a settlement, hoping to take his share before any real work is required. In all these cases, the problem is the same: Once you give the lawyer a financial stake in your case, he may begin to care more about his stake than about yours.

The final problem with contingency fee arrangements is that they can result in huge windfalls for lawyers. The typical justification for these "windfall fees" goes something like this: When a lawyer handles a matter on a contingency basis he may spend hundreds of hours on it. If he loses, he won't receive one cent of compensation for his time. The successful cases have to cover those that are unsuccessful. Most cases involving windfall fees, however, do not require hundreds of hours of work and the attorney's share of the award works out to hundreds of times what he could have charged on a flat fee basis or even at an hourly rate.

For all these reasons, you should avoid contingency fee arrangements whenever possible. *Never* hire an attorney on a contingency fee basis if you can afford to pay him at his hourly rate. If you do have to employ a contingency agreement—if, for example, the litigation threatens to drag on interminably—make sure you negotiate a multilevel fee that provides for a lower share if the case doesn't go to trial or if there's a premature settlement.

Contingency fees are usually appropriate (though seldom desirable) for the following kinds of activities:

- personal injury suits,
- wrongful death suits,
- other types of tort claims.

REFERRAL FEES

Referral fees are the fees you pay one lawyer for referring you to another. Typically, you go first to a generalist. He listens to your problem, then tells you what kind of specialist you need. The major problem with referral fees is that they're easily abused—and for years they were. The second lawyer usually paid the referring lawyer a kickback—which came not out of the second lawyer's fees, but out of the client's pocket.

Because of these and other abuses, all fifty states have now outlawed referral fees except when all of the following conditions are met:

- the client consents to the referral;
- the exact fee division between the lawyers is disclosed to the client;

- the fee division is proportionate to the services performed and responsibilities assumed by each lawyer;
- *the total fee doesn't exceed what the client would have had to pay if only one lawyer had been involved.*

Despite these statutory safeguards, you should beware of referrals and fee-splitting (another form of fee sharing between attorneys that is also subject to the above conditions). Although technically outlawed, a good deal of this activity still goes on under the guise of professional cooperation. Lawyers will recommend other lawyers solely on the basis of friendship, old school ties, or an informal reciprocal arrangement. The usual incentive for making these arrangements is not to serve the client better, but simply to make a little extra money.

If your lawyer insists on referring you to another lawyer, you should ask him the following questions:

- Why is he suggesting a referral?
- Why is he referring you to this particular lawyer?
- Can he personally recommend this lawyer? (Does he have firsthand experience of his work?)
- Does this lawyer have training or experience that he himself doesn't have?
- Will he receive any part of the fee you pay the other lawyer, and if so, how much?
- Will he receive his "cut" before or after the legal work is done?
- Will he continue to be involved in your legal affairs, and if so, to what extent? (How will the lawyers share the burdens and responsibilities of handling your case?)

RETAINERS AND REFRESHERS

A retainer is the money you pay the lawyer as an advance on his fee to cover out-of-pocket expenses. A refresher is an additional advance given from time to time. As a general rule, you should avoid lawyers who insist on these kinds of payments. Most lawyers don't. If yours does, it may be an indication that he doesn't trust you—unless the lawyer is young and just starting out, in which case he's got a good claim to a little money in advance. If not, then start looking for a lawyer whom you can trust *and* who trusts you.

THE BILL

A client in New York asked a local law firm to handle a case for him. The lawyer estimated that the job would cost about $25,000. A few months later, having heard nothing from the firm in the interim, the client received a bill for $105,000 based on fifteen pretrial motions, 335 hours of trial preparation, and a 103-page post-trial memorandum.

For years, the lawyer's bill has been a symbol of everything the average client resents about the legal profession. Impeccably typed on heavy, embossed stationery, it's a symbol of the profession's elitism. Terse and perfunctory, it's a symbol of the profession's guildish contempt for nonmembers. Exorbitant and unitemized, it's a symbol of the profession's preoccupation with profit. Bills that read simply "In the matter of ——— for services rendered" and then quote some staggering figure are still commonplace.

Not as commonplace as they used to be, however. The advent of advertising, legal clinics, and with them competition in the legal marketplace has brought cost-consciousness to legal consumers and a modicum of professional conscientiousness to the legal community. Even huge corporations that were once accustomed to paying millions of dollars in legal fees without blinking or asking for details are now demanding precise itemizations. "The mood of the legal consumer is changing," says a prominent legal journalist. "After years of having their clients chase them, lawyers are beginning to run after their clients. Accountability is going to kill some of the old perquisites." One of the most important of those old perquisites is the unitemized bill.

We said earlier that one of the main problems with the lawyer-client relationship is that the client has no adequate mechanism for monitoring the activities of the lawyer. This leads to misunderstanding and the possibility of abuse. In fact, ABA studies have shown that most of the complaints and criticisms clients lodge against lawyers result from the lawyer's failure to keep his clients well informed about what he's doing to solve their problems. The need for some form of regular communication is clear, both to keep the client informed and to protect the lawyer.

The bill provides that communication link. Legal consumers are discovering that it's the one sure-fire way of keeping track of their lawyers' activities. Most clients don't realize that most lawyers will give them a progress report over the telephone at no charge, so they refrain from calling for fear that the meter will start running. Because most clients are telephone shy, the bill is often their *only* line of communication with the lawyer. In the past, that has usually meant that there was no communication at all.

The Model Lawyer's Bill

Demand an itemized bill. If your lawyer refuses to provide it, find another lawyer.

Because the bill is often the only form of communication between lawyer and client, you should make sure it says as much as it can about your lawyer's activities. The bill should really be a progress report that also happens to deal with the subject of expenses. Its primary purpose should be informational, not financial.

Not surprisingly, lawyers and bar associations tend to resist the idea that a bill should be a progress report rather than a statement. This is partly because they don't like the record-keeping burdens it imposes, and partly because they simply don't like to have someone looking over their shoulders. As a prominent and candid Houston attorney put it: "Detailed billing has taken all of the fun out of practicing law. Besides, who wants to see an entry on their bill that reads 'leisurely three-martini lunch: $150.'"

You should overrule your lawyer's objections and insist on a bill that includes all of the information you need to know to stay well-informed about the progress of your legal affairs. If he refuses to provide such a bill, find another lawyer. You're paying the bills and you are completely within your rights to have them put in whatever reasonable form you choose.

What should the model lawyer's bill include? A good bill is a complete description of the lawyer's activities on your behalf. You should tell the lawyer in advance what elements you want the bill to contain and, if necessary, list those elements in the fee agreement which he signs. The bill should include:

- the name of the case or matter,
- the period which the bill covers,
- a list of activities with sufficient description to identify and differentiate them,
- when and where the services were rendered,
- the name of the person(s) who rendered the services,
- the duration of each activity and rate of payment,
- the total charge for services,
- all additional costs incurred during the billing period.

Name of case or matter. This is especially important if the same lawyer is handling more than one case or matter for you. Never let a lawyer aggregate his charges so that you don't know which costs relate to which case or matter.

Billing period. The bill should include the exact dates it covers, not simply "September" or, worst of all, "to date." Remember, a secondary purpose of this kind of "progress report" billing is to put pressure on your attorney to keep *his* records straight so you can keep your records straight.

List of activities. This is the most important item and you should take some care in specifying exactly what information you want included on the list. First, the activities should be described in sufficient detail to make them recognizable. It's not sufficient for the bill to say "made phone call." It should go on to specify who the lawyer talked with and what they talked about. For example: "Spoke to E.G. to arrange meeting to sign contract. Agreed on 9/1/83." The reason for including these details is that they help you assess the appropriateness of the charge for the service. If the phone call was merely to arrange a meeting date, it should not have taken more than a few minutes and the charge should therefore be only a few dollars.

When and where services were rendered. This can be part of the description of the service described above, but it should be specified for each activity listed. Remember, for example, that research in an office library is cheaper than research in an outside library and that, when a lawyer goes to court on your behalf, you have to pay for his travel time and expenses.

Who rendered services. The bill should specify who participated in a conference, who did the research for a particular memorandum, who filed papers, etc. If these tasks were done by support personnel in the firm—as they usually are—the bill doesn't need to list their names, but it should note their positions. This is to ensure that you're not charged the lawyer's rates for the work of paralegals and secretaries. If more than one lawyer is involved in your affairs, the bill should specify which of those lawyers actually did the work described.

Duration of activities. In addition to a description of each activity, who performed it, and when, the bill should tell you clearly how long the activity took and, if the activity is billed on an hourly basis, what the hourly rate for that activity is. Thus, a typical bill entry might read: "Research brief for case against E.G.; 10/5 to 10/8; paralegal, 15 hours @ $10/hour." An entry like this gives you all the information you need to evaluate the appropriateness of the service and the fee. The lawyer should also list how long his activities took and the hourly charge, if any, for each activity.

Total charge for services. After telling you what the activity was, who performed it, when, for how long, and at what rate, the bill should add all those up and tell you how much you've been charged for each activity. This may be simply a matter of arithmetic, but it will also give you a good index of where and how your money is being spent.

Additional costs. The bill should include an itemized list of any additional costs incurred during the billing period. The most common of these costs are filing fees, deposition costs, reporter fees, and other court costs.

What to Do If Your Lawyer Balks

This may seem like a great deal to ask your lawyer to provide, but you are justified in asking it. What do you do if, after you've hired him, your lawyer refuses to submit an itemized bill or neglects to make the bill conform to your instructions? You simply don't pay it. If a dispute follows, you've got his signature on a fee agreement (see Chapter 6) which specifies the form of the bill he has agreed to submit.

The Language of the Bill

It's now official: You don't have to accept the vague language that has characterized legal bills in the past. A New York federal district judge recently slashed a fee request of $200,000 to $5,000. The request, submitted by two New York attorneys, contained nothing but vague descriptions of what they'd done—phrases like "reviewed documents," "worked on records," "legal research," and similar formulations that are common in fee requests. If you run into such phrases in your lawyer's bill, you should react just as the judge did: Reject it.

8.
WHAT SHOULD YOU PAY?

If, as we've said, legal fees vary so much from city to city, state to state, case to case, lawyer to lawyer, how can you know what you should be paying? Because of the enormous variety of prices, and the fact that almost every case is different, it's very difficult to give sample prices. It is possible, however, to predict *ranges* in which most prices should fall. If the price a lawyer quotes you falls below the range, you're probably getting either a great bargain or an unrealistic estimate. If the quoted price exceeds the top end of the range, you're paying more than you should.

SAMPLE PRICES

Wills

A simple will should cost you about $75 to $150, depending on how "simple" it is. As soon as you start adding beneficiaries, dividing your property up into smaller pieces, putting conditions on who can inherit, and planning for contingencies, the bill starts going up. If you shop carefully enough, you can probably get a competent job on a no-frills will for as little as $35. One firm in upstate New York throws a will in free when it handles a house closing.

Trusts

A simple trust agreement (one that holds money or property for children until they come of age, for example) should cost $150 to $350. Again, if you want something more complicated, you'll have to pay for it. If the purpose of the trust is to avoid taxes, you'll probably want to consult a tax specialist—which can be expensive. Of course, if you have so much money that you *need* a tax shelter, you probably won't mind paying the premium. There are two major variables that affect the price of setting up a trust: the amount of money involved and the complexity of the terms of the trust. *Don't let a lawyer charge you a percentage of the money you plan to put in the trust to set it up.*

Incorporation

Simple incorporation should cost between $175 and $350 (plus disbursements for filing fees and the corporate kit). Again, this is assuming few complications and few assets. If you're starting a small business, for example, only a little money is at stake and you don't need a lot of paperwork. Don't let a lawyer convince you that you need a detailed and expensive incorporation because *someday* you'll be a big operation. That may be true, but the detailed and expensive incorporation work can wait until you're big enough to afford it. If you're in a particularly money-saving mood and you're *sure* there are no complications, you might even try one of the do-it-yourself incorporation "kits" now available.

Uncontested Divorce

There are two kinds of divorces: contested and uncontested. We can't give you a price range for contested divorces; there are just too many variables. An uncontested divorce, however, which involves little paperwork and less time, should cost between $150 and $500. This is a legal service, like will preparation and incorporation, in which there is intense price competition. So don't be surprised if you find a lawyer who'll quote you below this range. If the quote is significantly less, you should be suspicious. If it's more, you shouldn't pay it.

Separation Agreement

A separation agreement involves some time and work. But, assuming there isn't much property, the additional fee (on top of the fee for the uncontested divorce) should be between $150 and $400. You should be on your guard against lawyers who try to justify considerably higher fees by telling you how much more a contested divorce would have cost you. They think (or think they can convince you) that because the property settlement is saving you the expense of a divorce, they should charge you more. They shouldn't.

Real Estate

Real estate closings are usually handled on a percentage basis, that is, the fee is a percentage of the value of the property, usually about 1 percent. Oddly, the general practice is that the percentage rises along with the value of the property, even though selling an expensive property usually requires no more work on the lawyer's part. Some lawyers, however, will buck the system and handle a real estate closing for a set fee, ranging anywhere from $175 to $400. If you have an expensive piece of property and no complications, it will be worth your time and trouble to find a lawyer who'll take a set fee for his services.

Probate

Probate cases are another kind of case that lawyers often handle on a percentage basis. Again, the usual practice is to charge more for estates of greater value. This is one place where finding a lawyer who's willing to provide the service for a flat fee can save you a great deal of money. For example, it wouldn't be unusual for a lawyer to charge you 10 percent of an estate valued at $100,000, or $10,000. Another lawyer, however, may charge you a flat fee of $1,000, which is a significant saving.

Contracts

If you want a lawyer to read a contract or other agreement carefully to insure that it adequately protects your interest and says what you think it says, it should cost you about $50, depending on the length of the document. If you want the lawyer to *draft* the contract, the fee will be substantially higher. Beware, however. Many common transactions have standard contracts. The lawyer has books filled with these form contracts and it takes very little time to fill in the blanks. Even if the contract looks typed especially for you, it probably isn't. Many law offices now have machines and word processors that can turn out a document that looks tailor-made in about a minute and a half. Don't pay the lawyer's hourly rate for work done by a machine. If you're not doing something very special in the contract, the cost should be a small flat fee ($50 to $150), or else it should be based on the lawyer's hourly rate (but always less than one hour).

Civil Litigation

If you have a case that goes to court, there are two ways you can pay your lawyer: on a contingency fee basis, or on an hourly basis (see Chapter 7). If you can afford it, an hourly fee

basis is preferable. Hourly fees range from $35 per hour all the
way up to $250 or more per hour. It definitely is *not* the case
that the more a lawyer charges, the better lawyer he is. The
rate is one indication of the lawyer's experience, education, and
expertise, but it's not the only one. Besides, unless your case is
very unusual, unless it breaks new ground in a particular area
of the law, you probably don't *need* the rarified expertise of a
high-priced lawyer. In short, you don't need to pay more than
$45 or $50 per hour for most civil cases.

Criminal Matters

The price range for criminal lawyers is slightly below what it
is for civil litigation attorneys. Why? Because, for the most
part, there are fewer good lawyers specializing in criminal law.
That's good news for the bargain-hunter, but bad news for the
client looking for quality legal services. If your liberty is in
jeopardy, you may prefer a good defense to a cheap one. If you
do want quality, you'll have to pay for it. Because good
criminal defense attorneys are so rare, they command high
prices. You should expect to pay $50 to $75 for each hour of
their time.

NOTE: To defend you in a criminal case, a lawyer will often
ask for a retainer, an advance to help him cover his expenses.
The retainer can range from $100 to $1,000, depending on the
seriousness of the charge—and, frankly, on how rich you are
and how well-known the lawyer is. If you're not rich and the
lawyer suspects that he might have trouble collecting his fee
after the trial is over, he may ask for what's called an "artful
retainer," which is a retainer large enough to cover almost all of
the anticipated expenditures involved in the defense. In other
words, full payment in advance.

As soon as your lawyer sets foot in the courtroom, the fees
start to soar. In fact, most lawyers will start charging you at a
higher rate as soon as they step out of their office on their way
toward the courtroom. How much a lawyer charges you for a

court appearance depends on a variety of factors, especially the seriousness of the charge, the amount of money at stake, the nature of the courtroom proceeding (a motion is less expensive than a trial), and, as always, the lawyer's reputation. Legal legend has it that Edward Bennett Williams, the Washington, D.C., criminal attorney, charges $10,000 for every day he spends in court.

A more reasonable fee, assuming you're not an underworld kingpin or a senator in trouble, is between $250 and $350 for a court appearance. That's for a matter in which the stakes are relatively low. For a complex civil suit over large amounts of money, or a criminal trial in which you're facing a long prison term, you should expect to pay in the neighborhood of $750 to $1,500 per day. That's a great deal of money, but prison (and poverty) are ugly prospects.

ALTERNATIVES TO LEGAL FEES

Most people think legal fees, like death and taxes, are unavoidable. Until recently, that was essentially true. In the past ten years, however, several alternatives have appeared. If you're really interested in cutting your legal bills, you should consider one of the following alternatives to traditional pay-as-you-go legal fees:

- legal aid services,
- prepaid legal service plans,
- prepaid legal expense insurance,
- public interest law services.

Legal Aid Services

Legal aid offices have been set up in most areas of the country, especially metropolitan areas, to provide legal services to those who couldn't afford them otherwise. There is considerable variety among legal aid offices in funding sources, methods of operation, eligibility requirements, kinds of legal services provided, and quality of legal services. Because they deal primarily with the problems of the poor, however, and operate on limited budgets, these services are usually understaffed and lack the funds necessary to handle anything more than the simplest and most routine legal problems.

Prepaid Legal Service Plans

Some labor unions, corporations, cooperatives, and consumer organizations offer prepaid legal service plans in which members can take their legal problems to a designated lawyer or lawyers free of charge. Lawyers are hired to deal exclusively with the problems of the plan subscribers. Currently, about 2,500,000 people are on such plans. Because the plans vary greatly in coverage and operation, you should ask some questions before subscribing to one available to you. The most important questions to ask are:

- How old is the plan?
- How many members does it cover?
- What legal services are provided free, which ones are extra?
- How are lawyers selected for the plan?
- How many lawyers are available at any given time to deal with members' problems? (What is the lawyer-to-member ratio? One to five hundred is good, anything higher is suspicious.)
- What is the grievance procedure if the client has a dispute with a lawyer under the plan? (If there isn't such a procedure, don't join.)

Prepaid Legal Expense Insurance

Legal expense insurance works more like traditional medical insurance; that is, you pay a premium (or your company deducts a premium from your salary) and you're reimbursed if you incur any legal expenses. The major advantage of such a policy is that it allows you to choose your own legal counsel. The major disadvantage is that it may not cover some kinds of legal expenses or the full legal expenses incurred. Like medical coverage, legal coverage of this kind varies greatly from company to company, from policy to policy. While it is, in general, more flexible than prepaid legal service plans, it's also more expensive.

Public Interest Law Services

There are a number of organizations, both local and national, that take cases without charging a fee because they involve important public policy issues. If you're lucky enough to have a case that fits the "agenda" of one of these organizations, you may get a free ride all the way to the Supreme Court. Of course, the disadvantage of these services is that they're available *only* if your case relates to public policy issues such as the environment, land use, race or sex discrimination, voting rights, employment discrimination, consumer protection, mental health, civil liberties, education, or some other constitutional right.

RESPONDING TO ADVERTISEMENTS

If you shop around and compare prices for legal services, you'll soon discover that the lowest prices are offered, almost invariably, by so-called legal clinics and announced in bold-faced newspaper ads and television commercials. Despite the low prices, however, many people are reluctant to respond to legal advertisements. They're not used to the idea of a lawyer advertising a "special" on uncontested divorces, and they have doubts about the integrity, professionalism, or competence of any attorney who puts himself on the screen like a car salesman.

How well-founded are these doubts? Are rates the only thing that "cut-rate" legal clinics cut? Are you putting your legal interests on the line by responding to an advertisement in the paper or on television? Is advertising really a boon to the consumer or just a new way for dishonest lawyers to rip off an unsuspecting public?

There's no doubt that advertising has had a profound—and beneficial—effect on the cost of legal services. It has allowed firms to provide and publicize cheaper alternative forms of legal services, and thereby to create the kind of competitive pressure that forces other lawyers, many of whom don't advertise, to cut their fees in order to meet the competition. "It wouldn't make much sense to advertise fees that were much higher than those quoted by the guy down the street," says Thomas Hoffman, a New York City lawyer. Hoffman is a case in point. When advertising was legalized, he cut his charge for an uncontested divorce in half: from $500 to $250.

Can You Trust a Lawyer Who Advertises?

When advertising was first seriously proposed, the bar associations attacked it mercilessly as a denigration of the profession and a consumer nightmare. Some people found that position ironic. As legal journalist Stephen Brill pointed out at the time, "they [the bar associations] are in the awkward position of maligning the profession in order to protect it. They claim that [advertising] would be abused by all the crooked lawyers out there."

Advertising has not proven to be the consumer rip-off its opponents feared. "We keep a very sharp eye out for such things," says the ABA's Jeffrey Thumond, "and as far as I know, there hasn't been a single grievance filed by a client who answered an ad." Even though the legal profession's grievance procedures are notoriously faulty, that's a remarkable record.

Tips for Shopping for the Best Price

The relatively good record of lawyers who advertise should not lull you into a false sense of security. Whenever you respond to a newspaper or television advertisement, you should be wary, whether the ad is for records, vegetable choppers, or uncontested divorces. Here are some precautions you can take to insure that you don't become one of the first casualties of cut-rate legal services.

• *Shop around.* This rule applies no matter how you're doing your shopping, but it's particularly important if you're going through advertisements. If you take the time to look, chances are you'll find at least one other lawyer advertising the same price. That will give you a chance to compare other factors such as experience, personality, reputation, etc., before choosing one lawyer over another. Also, you're likely to find other lawyers who may not advertise low rates, but are willing to lower their prices to meet the competition.

• *Find out what's included for the fee advertised.* For example, does the advertised fee include all the possible additional charges such as court fees, filing fees, witness or recording expenses, etc.? If it doesn't, find out how much they will add to the total cost. Because these charges can sometimes amount to as much as the fee itself, what looks like a bargain at first may turn out to be a rip-off.

• *Ask about the lawyer's hourly rates.* If charges beyond the advertised fee are involved, the lawyer should tell you what his hourly rate is. If he doesn't, it's fair to assume he has something to hide. But you should ask about hourly rates even if it doesn't look as though your business will involve any additional work, because you can never be sure that things will go the way you or your lawyer expect them to.

• *Ask how much of a retainer the lawyer will require.* One lawyer may advertise a relatively low charge but require that you pay it all up front. Another may allow you to pay in installments. Another may ask for only a small deposit at the beginning and the rest when he completes the work. In general, you should always pay a lawyer after he has finished his job, not before.

• *Find out what happens to the money you've paid if you drop the case, if the lawyer drops out of the case, or if you reach a settlement.* The lawyer normally should keep no more than half of the retainer if the case comes to a premature end. The same rule applies if you're only asking him to work on an incorporation. If you decide halfway through that you don't want to incorporate, the lawyer should be willing to give you a portion of the money back.

• *Don't be satisfied with vague assurances or evasive answers to any of these questions.* The best thing about competition is that it gives the consumer choices. If a lawyer doesn't respond quickly and willingly to your questions, choose another lawyer.

9.
NEGOTIATING A CONTINGENCY FEE

A contingency fee is a fee which your lawyer receives only when and *if* he wins your case. If he does, he gets a percentage of the money (damages) the court awards you.

Because no money (except for the retainer, if there is one) changes hands until the case is completed, many clients don't bother to negotiate further once the lawyer has agreed to take the case on a contingency basis. That is a serious mistake. The same rule applies to contingency fee arrangements as to any other kind of fee arrangement: Negotiate everything. The primary difference in the contingency fee context is that you'll be negotiating a percentage figure instead of a flat dollar amount or an hourly rate. Because there is a growing tendency for lawyers to abuse the contingency fee arrangement, here are some rules to keep in mind:

- Never agree to a flat percentage contingency fee.
- Never agree to any rate over 33⅓ percent.
- Never accept a given rate as 'standard.'
- In all negotiations, remember that contingency fees are an invitation to abuse.

- If your lawyer is working on a contingency basis, monitor his activity more closely.

WHY CONTINGENCY FEES?

Contingency fees were once the Great Client Hope. When first introduced thirty years ago, they were hailed by legal reformers as a great step in opening up the legal system to lower and middle class clients who could not otherwise afford to pay for justice. They were to be the great legal equalizer. In contrast, the established bar considered them a cheap gimmick and greeted them with skeptical distaste thinly disguised as tolerance. Despite maxims and mottoes to the contrary, the established bar had never been comfortable with the idea of legal power in the hands of the lower classes.

Like most promising inventions, however, contingency fees have proven to be a mixed blessing. There are those in the bar, like New York attorney Stuart Speiser, who still believe that contingency fees represent a great step forward in the legal system. In glowing terms, Speiser describes the lawyer who works on a contingency basis as an "advocate who carries a client on his shoulders by providing and financing services that most individual clients cannot afford—services which put an average individual on an equal litigation footing with a corporate giant."

The rhetoric is partly justified. Contingency fees have made possible a number of suits, often by poor clients against corporate giants, that wouldn't have been possible otherwise. If you are among the many would-be clients who have a major claim but can't afford to pay a lawyer's hourly rate, a contingency fee arrangement may be the only way you can have your day in court.

Is a Contingency Fee Right for You?

Until recently, contingency fees, like army uniforms, came in only one size: too big. The standard percentage—everywhere—was 33⅓ percent. The only flexibility was upward: You could occasionally find 40 and 50 percent rates. "One can drop into just about any American city or town," said Raoul Kennedy, a San Francisco lawyer, "knowing ahead of time that death and taxes are not the only things that can be counted on with certainty. In addition to being able to find a Coke and a Big Mac, one also knows that . . . if one is injured, the lawyer's contingent fee will be at least 33⅓ percent."

Some changes are in the wind, however. Partly due to widespread condemnation of "windfall" awards, partly due to a glut of hungry young lawyers, partly due to public outrage, and partly due to internal criticism, the 33⅓ standard, like the gold standard before it, has begun to crumble. The upshot is that you're now on firm ground if you challenge a lawyer's request for a flat one-third fee.

In fact, it is *unethical* for a lawyer not to inform you that there are less expensive alternatives to the one-third contingency fee arrangement in cases of personal injury. The American Bar Association Code of Professional Responsibility says: "A lawyer should be mindful that many persons who desire to employ him may have had little experience with fee charges of lawyers, and for this reason he should explain fully to such persons the reason for the particular fee arrangement that he proposes." The Code also says that lawyers "generally should decline to accept employment on a contingent fee basis by one who is able to pay a reasonable fixed fee."

Also, once you have agreed to a contingency fee, remember that it should be reasonable in light of the facts of your case. Do not agree to a one-third contingency fee because your lawyer tells you it's "standard." If he insists that the rate is not flexible, quote him the following passage from the U.S. Court of Appeals for the Seventh Circuit: ". . . although an attorney may contract with a client for a contingent fee . . . his right to do so is not unrestrained . . . The right to contract is limited to a 'reasonable' contingent fee."

NEGOTIATING THE CONTINGENCY FEE RATE

If there is no longer a standard rate, then how do you determine what the rate should be? A variety of factors must be considered:

Does the defendant dispute liability? This is the most important of the factors affecting a contingency fee. If the defendant doesn't dispute liability, then there is little more for your lawyer to do than file a complaint, appear in court, hold a few conferences, and talk with you on the phone. That's about it. Most serious abuses of contingency fee arrangements occur when the lawyer takes a third of the award in a case that never went to trial.

Of course, it's not always easy to know in advance whether the defendant will dispute liability, in which case there are two things you can do to protect yourself. First, take advantage of several free initial conferences with lawyers to get their sense of whether the case will be disputed. If that doesn't work, make sure that your fee agreement provides for a significant reduction in the lawyer's percentage if the defendant doesn't dispute liability.

What are the chances that the case will go to trial? This question is related to the question of whether the defendant will dispute liability. If the defendant doesn't dispute liability, you can be sure that the case will not go to trial. However, if the defendant does dispute liability, it doesn't necessarily mean that the case *will* go to trial. There is always the possibility of a settlement. Often a defendant can't, for tactical reasons, concede liability, but he can always negotiate to settle a suit.

The problem here is the same as before. How do you know what the chances of going to court are? If you ask the lawyer you're bargaining with, he has every incentive to exaggerate the risk of a prolonged and costly court fight as a way of justifying a larger percentage of the award. The solution here is also the same as before. Negotiate a two-level percentage: a higher percentage if the case goes to trial, a lower percentage if it doesn't.

How much of the lawyer's work and time is likely to be involved? The answer to this question depends somewhat on the answers to the previous questions. Obviously, if your lawyer has to fight the defendant's lawyer or has to prepare for court, the case will involve far more of his time than if the defendant chooses not to dispute or to settle. Some cases, however, don't require great expenditures of time on the part of counsel; others are relatively simple in law, in fact, or in both. You shouldn't pay a lawyer a whopping share of your award if he did relatively little work, even if that work involved a trial. There's nothing magical about the courtroom; it doesn't lend validity to any fee. It's true, as a general rule, that time in court requires more preparation and is therefore more expensive. But it is by no means written in stone.

The best way to get a sense of how much time the case will require is to go to more than one lawyer and ask them, without mentioning the possibility of a contingency fee, for an estimate of the number of hours the case would require if you paid them on an hourly basis.

How much money is involved? One of the justifications for the contingency fee is that, by giving the lawyer a stake in the winnings, the arrangement gives him an incentive to win as much as possible. That may be true, but it doesn't justify large fees for work which, billed *any* other way, would have earned much less. If you stand to win a great deal of money, the percentage should be lower than if the potential winnings are small.

Many lawyers don't agree: They prefer to charge *more* when more money is at stake. For example, it is common to charge a higher percentage of the selling price for closing a real estate transaction if the property is worth more money. Lawyers understandably like this kind of arithmetic; but there's no reason you should buy it. If a lawyer you speak to refuses to give you a lower percentage figure on a larger amount of money, you can find one who will. Another possibility is to propose, again, a two-level arrangement whereby the lawyer's percentage will be less on any award over a certain amount.

Are there other plaintiffs? The existence of other plaintiffs will affect all of the factors listed so far. As a rule, the more plaintiffs there are, the more likely it is that the defendant will dispute liability. On the other hand, if the defendant doesn't dispute liability, a crowd of plaintiffs will probably encourage more active (and often more generous) pursuit of settlements.

If the defendant does put up a fight, numerous plaintiffs can often band together to press their case, resulting in less work for each individual plaintiff's attorney. Or, in some cases where there are a number of potential plaintiffs, a particularly sympathetic one will be chosen to litigate the key issues while the others await the outcome. In this case—unless you're the chosen plaintiff—your lawyer should have little to do but stand and watch. It would be difficult for you to know these things in advance, but the existence of other plaintiffs should put you on guard when you negotiate the fee agreement.

A NEW STANDARD FOR CONTINGENCY FEES: THE SLIDING SCALE

As an alternative to the two-level type of fee mentioned above, you should try negotiating a so-called sliding scale fee. Sliding scale arrangements are not new in the profession. Smart clients have been using them for years, but primarily in transactions involving real estate where the fee is calculated as a percentage of the value of the property. In the context of personal injury cases, they're designed to eliminate the dreaded windfalls that "lawyer-enterpreneurs" are always looking for—contingency fees sometimes as high as 50 percent.

It may seem complicated at first, but the principle behind sliding scale fees is beautiful in its simplicity: The higher the amount of the recovery, the lower the lawyer's percentage. A typical scale would look like this:

The lawyer will receive
    25% of the first $10,000;
    20% of any amount from $10,000 to $20,000;
    15% of any amount from $20,000 to $50,000;
    10% of any amount from $50,000 to $100,000;
     5% of any amount over $100,000.

You can make an arrangement like this even more sensitive by formulating different scales for different possible outcomes—for example, one scale of percentages if the case is settled, a different one (with higher percentages) if the case goes to trial. In this way, the fee agreement can be made responsive not only to the size of the award, but also to the other factors mentioned above: the number of plaintiffs, the lawyer time required, the chance of going to trial, and the defendant's willingness to dispute liability.

The scale above would be appropriate for a personal injury or wrongful death suit that's settled without a trial. If the same case did go to trial, however, an appropriate alternative fee scale would be:

The lawyer will receive
    33% of the first $10,000;
    25% of any amount from $10,000 to $20,000;
    20% of any amount from $20,000 to $50,000;
    15% of any amount from $50,000 to $100,000;
    10% of any amount over $100,000.

If you don't think the difference is worth the effort, you should consider the case of a New Hampshire man who won a $150,000 judgment against a trucking company for injuries he sustained when one of the company trucks dumped a load of gravel on his car as he stopped at a red light. His lawyer told him that his case would be tough and therefore demanded 40 percent of the "profits." Knowing no better, the man agreed. When the money was divided, the lawyer walked away with $60,000 *plus* expenses, leaving the victim—in a wheelchair— with only slightly more than half. If he had negotiated the sliding scale fee arrangement outlined above, he could have kept almost $125,000. If the case had been *settled* for the same amount prior to trial, he would have received $134,000—a $50,000 bonus for taking the time to negotiate.

Sliding scale fee arrangement can be used in a variety of cases that have nothing to do with personal injury, or even jury trials. Any time a lawyer asks for a percentage fee—and you decide that such a fee is in your best interest—negotiate a sliding scale. That way, the more money the transaction costs you, the less money you'll have to pay the lawyer. For example, if a lawyer asks a percentage fee for real estate transfers, especially buying and selling a house, the "going rate" is 1 percent of the sale price. But, here again, the rate is flexible. Here is a sliding scale arrangement for such transactions:

The lawyer will receive
    1% of the first $20,000;
    ¾% of any amount from $20,000 to $40,000;
    ½% of any amount from $40,000 to $60,000;
    ¼% of any amount over $60,000.

You can negotiate the same kind of scale if you have a collection case or if you want the lawyer to handle the estate of someone recently deceased. Wherever they're used, sliding scale fee arrangements invariably save clients thousands of dollars in unnecessary—and unearned—legal fees.

THINGS TO REMEMBER

Negotiating contingency fees is harder than negotiating other kinds of fees because you have to plan for a number of different possibilities: The defendant may roll over and concede everything, or he may fight like a street cat; the case may be joined by other plaintiffs, or you may have to go it alone; the lawyer may withdraw, or you may fire him; the case may turn out to be time-consuming and complex, or it may turn out to be a breeze; it may go to trial, or it may end in a settlement; there may be a small award, or there may be a huge award.

If you were deciding on an appropriate fee *after* the case was completed, all of these factors would go into the calculation. With contingency fees, however, you have to consider them before the case is even begun. So negotiations present some special problems.

• *Be sure to estimate what the total fee would be if you figured it on an hourly basis.* This will require the cooperation of the lawyer and a great deal of guesswork. But an experienced lawyer should be able to give you a roughly accurate idea of the time involved after you've given him a detailed description of the case. Be sure to ask for time estimates assuming the case is settled early, settled late, or taken to trial. Put these estimates together with the lawyer's assessment of the chances of settlement and decide whether it would be cheaper to go ahead and pay him on an hourly basis. Of course, if you haven't got the money, this option isn't really available. But don't let him know that. There's always the option of going to another lawyer.

• *Negotiate the retainer.* When it comes to negotiation, you should treat the retainer exactly as you would treat a flat fee or hourly rate. If your case is good, the lawyer shouldn't insist on a retainer. In general, they're a kind of insurance, like a bond. A struggling young lawyer might have to insist on a retainer to stay in the black while he works on your case. If a successful lawyer insists on a retainer, however, it generally means one of three things: He doesn't think much of your case, he's trying to discourage your business, or he doesn't trust you. In any case, you should find another lawyer.

• *Do a little preliminary exploring of the settlement possibilities.* Before agreeing to pursue a claim on a contingency fee basis, find out what your opponents are willing to offer as a settlement. You may end up with more if you take the settlement and avoid paying a whopping percentage of the final award to your lawyer. Your lawyer should tell you if hiring him will actually reduce your take. But beware, many are not so forthcoming. A naive plaintiff in Los Angeles, California, was offered a $50,000 settlement only days after being injured in a car accident. She went to a lawyer and asked whether she should accept the offer. The lawyer convinced her to sign a fee agreement giving him a third of any recovery and two days later accepted the $50,000 settlement.

• *Find out what the limits on contingency fees are in your state and in your kind of case.* Many states put a variety of limits on contingency fees. They limit by statute the percentage that lawyers can charge, prohibit the use of contingency fees altogether in certain kinds of cases, and place conditions on the negotiation of a contingency fee. The same is true of some federal laws. Consult your local or state bar association for the limitations on contingency fees in your state. Or, when you begin discussing fees with the lawyer, ask him to explain the limitations. All you have to do is demonstrate that you know such limits exist and he'll be sure to abide by them.

• *Resist any effort to "adjust" the fee arrangements after the case is concluded.* A lawyer may suggest that you allow for an increase in the total fees if the services are more complicated or consume more time than he originally estimated. If you employed a sliding scale fee arrangement and thought it through carefully, this situation shouldn't arise. If it does, however—if he suggests changing the percentages used in the scale—you should be suspicious of any such request. It may just mean that he intentionally underestimated the time and expense, or the likelihood of a trial, or the chances of a settlement in order to get you to give him your business.

If you decide to include in the fee agreement a provision or a separate scale that gives the lawyer a higher percentage if he ends up doing a lot of extra work, be sure you also include a provision or separate scale that applies if the case takes less work or less time than originally estimated, and gives you the right to reduce the amount of the fee accordingly. It's a two-way street. If the lawyer balks, find another lawyer.

• *When your lawyer is working on a contingency basis, you should monitor his activity very closely.* We said before that any percentage or contingency fee offers the greatest potential for lawyers to cheat clients and receive excessive profits at the clients' expense. There are other ways in which a contingency fee arrangement can adversely affect your interests. If, for example, after looking into your case more closely, the lawyer decides that there is not much chance of a sizeable recovery, he is apt to quietly drop or at least curtail work on your case. After all, you're not paying him by the hour. For the same reason, a lawyer might become overanxious to settle your case and realize at least *some* money before he puts more of his time into it. In both instances, you should be following his activity closely enough to know if his interests and your interests have parted company. That, of course, is the time to consult another lawyer.

• *Remember to provide for the possibility that the lawyer will leave your case before a settlement or award.* Any fee agreement should address the possibility that the lawyer will withdraw from the case before it's completed, either on his own motion, or at the request of the client. But under a contingency agreement, because the lawyer isn't paid until the case is completed, you should take special care in deciding how to pay the lawyer if he leaves the case.

10.
WORKING WITH A LAWYER: THE ATTORNEY-CLIENT RELATIONSHIP IN ACTION

Once the fee agreement has been negotiated, you should begin immediately to establish and maintain a smooth and effective working relationship with your lawyer. A good attorney-client relationship is an ongoing affair which requires the attention and conscientiousness of the served no less than the servant. The best way to insure a smooth, supportive, and successful relationship with a lawyer is to know what you should expect of him and what he expects of you.

WHAT YOU SHOULD EXPECT FROM YOUR LAWYER

Lawyers, like doctors, accept certain duties when they're licensed to practice. If a lawyer you hire violates one of these duties, you can withhold his fees, discharge him, bring disciplinary action against him, or sue him for malpractice. Some (though not all) of a lawyer's duties are among the nine "canons," or rules, proposed in the new Rules of Professional

Conduct currently under consideration by the American Bar Association. You are within your legal rights to expect the following:

* confidentiality,
* no conflicts of interest,
* reasonable competence,
* advocacy,
* honesty,
* respect for your other rights.

Confidentiality

Lawyers are prohibited from revealing what you tell them in the context of the lawyer-client relationship. This prohibition applies no matter what you tell them, no matter how embarrassing or heinous it may be. Otherwise, you wouldn't be able to speak to them freely. And without that, they wouldn't be able to represent your interests fully.

The duty of confidentiality extends beyond the lawyer himself to all the people in his office: the paralegal who researches your case, the secretary who types your letters, even the janitors who clean the office where your files are kept. The lawyer is responsible for the actions of all these subordinates. If any of them divulges damaging information, the lawyer himself has breached his duty of confidentiality.

The duty of confidentiality also extends in time beyond the boundaries of the lawyer-client relationship. Even if you should later dismiss him and hire another lawyer, he remains duty-bound.

There are, however, some limits on the duty of confidentiality. For example, if a client discusses a legal matter with his lawyer in the presence of a third person, he may lose his right to confidentiality. In addition, a lawyer is permitted to disclose client confidences:

- when, by so doing, he can prevent the commission of a future crime;
- when he convinces the client that to disclose confidences is in the client's best interest and the client consents;
- when he can't represent the client adequately without disclosing the confidence;
- when he must disclose the confidence in order to collect his fee;
- when he must disclose the confidence in order to protect himself or the other members of his firm from the client's charges of wrongdoing.

As you can see, these exceptions to the rule of confidentiality tend to buttress the claim, often made by the legal profession's critics, that lawyers put profit before ethics. There's no doubt that these exceptions favor the lawyer's purse over the client's interest. When they reveal their darkest secrets, most clients don't realize that the lawyer can repeat anything they say in order to collect his fee or defend himself in a malpractice suit. A simpler and more honest statement of the rule of confidentiality might be: If it's in the lawyer's interest to keep your confidence (or if it doesn't affect him one way or the other—which is usually the case), he will abide by it; if it's not, he won't.

No Conflicts of Interest

Avoiding conflicts of interest is, in fact, much more difficult than it may seem. For example, if after years of sharing the same family lawyer, you and your spouse decide to divorce and both of you want that lawyer to represent you, there's a conflict. If after using a certain firm to handle your business affairs, you have some legal difficulties with a business associate who's represented by the same firm, again, there's a conflict of interest. And it's a conflict even if the two of you are represented by different attorneys in the same firm.

There are three things a lawyer can do if he's cornered into a conflict of interest. He can tell both you and the other party about the conflict, then get your consent to continue to represent you both; he can stop representing one of you; or he can stop representing both of you. In any event, you should always hear about the conflict of interest first from the lawyer himself. If you hear about it first from someone else, your lawyer has either been negligent or deceitful and should be discharged.

Despite the obvious temptation to do so, you should avoid getting into a business relationship with your lawyer. That may be a particularly hard injunction to follow, especially when your lawyer agrees to waive his substantial fees in exchange for a share of the profits. But any such business relationship raises serious conflict of interest problems. How can a lawyer represent you in business dealings when his interest and yours, as business partners, may not coincide? If you insist on joint ventures with your lawyer, you should hire another lawyer to handle the venture's legal affairs.

Finally, if for any reason you think your lawyer may have a conflict of interest, you should immediately demand in writing a statement that he does not.

Reasonable Competence

There's no rule which requires a lawyer to be brilliant. There is, however, a rule which requires him to be competent. If instead he demonstrates gross incompetence, you have grounds for a malpractice suit. Unfortunately, competence isn't a difficult standard to satisfy. Generally, a lawyer is considered competent if he knows the "plain and elementary principles of law" commonly known by well-informed lawyers; does research to find out the more obscure principles of law with which he isn't familiar; and makes good decisions based on an intelligent assessment of the facts.

(For more information on what constitutes competence, see

Chapter 5, Choosing a Lawyer, and Chapter 14, Legal
Malpractice.)

Advocacy

The American legal system is an adversary system: You have
a lawyer and your adversary has a lawyer. Both lawyers
represent their clients to the best of their abilities, regardless of
their personal feelings about the right or wrong of the matter.
The lawyers are paid to represent their clients, not judge them.

The American idea is that, if both sides are well represented
by articulate and aggressive advocates, the "justice" of the
matter will somehow magically emerge. And indeed—occasionally—the system works that way. More often, however, it
doesn't. A more common scenario is that one party has a
brilliant lawyer, the other party has a dunce, and, invariably,
the former wins. Unfortunately, the imbalance doesn't always
fall on the side of justice.

The point is simple: If you are to have any chance of
wringing justice from the American legal system, your lawyer
must be an effective advocate. This isn't just a gentlemanly
courtesy he owes you under the Code of Professional Responsibility, it's an essential part of making the system work as well
as it can. It shouldn't matter what he happens to think of you or
of your claim. If for any reason you begin to doubt the vigor
and commitment of your lawyer's advocacy, you should start
looking for a replacement.

Honesty

In the words of the Code of Professional Responsibility, "a
lawyer shall not . . . engage in conduct involving dishonesty,
fraud, deceit, or misrepresentation." Some lawyers obey this
injunction; others do not.

Your lawyer's duty to be honest and fair is called a

"fiduciary" duty: He can't take advantage of the relationship in any way that will benefit him and harm you. For example:

- If you tell your barber about your new invention, nothing except decency keeps him from taking a patent out on it before you do. If you mention the same invention to your lawyer and he takes out a patent, you can sue.
- If you pay your maid a month in advance, the money is hers to do with as she likes. If you pay your lawyer a year in advance (i.e., you give him a retainer), he must put the money in an interest-bearing account until he actually earns it—and he is obliged to give you the interest.

Respect for Your Other Rights

In addition to the duties imposed by the Canons of Professional Ethics, the lawyer has a duty to respect certain client rights which are the combined product of tradition, courtesy, and common sense.

- *Right of access.* You have the right of access to all of your records and files. You may have to make a special appointment with your lawyer to see those files, but he can't use scheduling difficulties to obstruct your access to them.
- *Right to written statements.* All important negotiations with your lawyer should be transacted—or at least confirmed—in writing so you have records for your files. Such records are useful under any circumstances, but particularly if difficulties should arise.
- *Right to plain English.* In many states, you even have a formal right to written communications in *plain English*. These states have passed what are called "Plain English" statutes which require that lawyers avoid jargon wherever possible in favor of simple understandable English.
- *Right to information.* Edward A. Schwartz, general counsel

for Digital Corporation, says, "Some general counsels get an ego trip from a large bill from a prestigious firm. But the trend is changing. We ask for a complete breakdown of all our bills. A lot of firms don't like that, but if a firm won't do it we won't use them." You should follow suit.

• *Right to participate.* You have a right to participate in all decisions affecting your legal affairs. A good lawyer should lay out the various options available to you, explain the advantages and disadvantages of each, offer his opinion, then let you make the final decision.

• *Right to discharge.* You have an absolute right to discharge your lawyer, with or without cause, at any time. If you discharge him without cause, however, you owe him reasonable compensation for the services he has rendered up to the time of discharge.

WHAT YOUR LAWYER SHOULD EXPECT FROM YOU

Good legal representation is a team effort. The lawyer has to do his best, but so does the client. Here are some of the things you can do to maintain good relations with your lawyer and to advance your own legal cause.

Complete Cooperation

To do his job effectively, your attorney needs your full and unhesitant cooperation. Think of it as simple reciprocity. The following are some of the most common—and most appreciated—forms of client cooperation.

• *Prompt payment.* Just as you expect your attorney to charge reasonable fees, he expects you to pay them reasonably soon. If you can't pay him promptly, at least inform him of your inability to do so and try to work out alternate arrangements.

• *Availability.* Your lawyer should be available when you need him; and you should be available when he needs you. You should never give your attorney the sense that your legal affairs are less important to you than they are to him.

• *Confidentiality*. Most clients think of this as a duty that applies only to the lawyer. That may be technically true: There are no canons of ethics for clients. But your lawyer's obligation to keep your dealings confidential is meaningless if you don't respect that confidentiality as well.

• *Candor*. When a lawyer asks you to describe your problem, tell him the *whole* story. Don't hold back details because they're legally or personally embarrassing. Don't omit things you think your lawyer doesn't want to hear because they might hurt your case. It may be difficult to tell a divorce lawyer that you've been cheating on your spouse, or to tell a tax lawyer that you didn't report all your income last year; but you'll hurt your case more by hiding facts than by revealing them. Besides, your lawyer won't be shocked. Unless your secret is particularly dark, chances are he's heard it before. What *will* shock him is if you wait until the day before a trial begins to share a particularly damaging fact; or—worse—if you wait and let your adversary bring it out in the courtroom. Nothing will undermine your case (or your lawyer's respect for you) more than lack of candor.

Personal Initiative

While your legal problem may be the most pressing matter in your life at the moment, it probably doesn't have the same priority in your lawyer's life. That's a good reason to stay actively involved in the case yourself. Don't let your lawyer take a major step without consulting you first, laying out the options, and explaining each one in detail. Don't sign a document, make a binding statement, or enter a courtroom without an adequate briefing. A bad lawyer will resent your meddling; a good one will appreciate your concern.

• *Keep some control over the case*. It's your case, too. If you think it might be helpful to take some action yourself (negotiating a settlement, for example), feel free to do so after consulting with your lawyer. Because you know your affairs better than he does, you may think of issues and approaches that wouldn't occur to him. Just be sure to coordinate your efforts.

• *Keep him informed.* Never do anything that concerns your case without telling your lawyer first. If you wait until after you do it, the costs of rectifying any possible errors will be far greater than those of asking the lawyer's advice in the first place.

• *Maintain schedules.* Lengthy delays are a major problem in the American legal system, but you must not make it worse. If your lawyer asks you to assemble documents or prepare certain materials by a specific date, he probably has a deadline in mind. If you fall behind in your schedule, he'll fall behind in his and your legal affairs will be delayed. Delay, of course, will cost you money as well as time.

Keeping Informed

It's up to you to stay well informed about your legal affairs. The idea that the lawyer is a shepherd and the client a trusting sheep is so deeply engrained in our society that even the best lawyers rarely bother to keep their clients informed of the details of a case. And of course, many clients would prefer to leave all the worrisome details to their lawyers and follow them, quietly bleating, through the pastures of the law. A *good* client, however, stays well informed. He wants to make sure that, if something goes wrong, he's aware of it.

• *Obtain copies.* Lawyers rarely bother to send their clients copies of important documents. After all, they're written in a legal language that few clients can understand. That may be true, but you can probably understand enough of the document to get the gist of it, and there's no other way to stay on top of the case.

• *Ask questions.* Your lawyer is your employee. You've hired him to take care of *your* case. You have a right, therefore, to ask him how it's developing. He should be willing to give you periodic briefings on your case, including the steps he has taken, the tactics he plans to use, and his current assessment of your prospects. These briefings may cost him time and you money, but only a well-informed client can contribute meaningfully to his own defense.

• *Call regularly.* You should be in regular contact with your lawyer. Even if he hasn't specifically requested information from you, he should be aware that you're concerned. Of course, if your expressions of concern are too frequent, they may interrupt his schedule, irritate him, and cost you money. But you should never let too long a period go by without making contact. How frequent is too frequent and how long is too long? In general, it depends on whether your case is long-term or short-term. If it's long-term—lasting more than a few months—you should call at least every two or three weeks. If it's short-term—lasting only a few weeks—once a week is not too often.

Record Keeping

A good client, like a good lawyer, keeps complete and careful records of his legal affairs. Good record keeping is an ongoing rather than a periodic process. It requires that you develop the right habits and observe them attentively. The effort will be well rewarded, however, especially if any difficulty should arise between you and your lawyer.

• *Write it down.* When your lawyer tells you something important, or you learn some important information relevant to your case, write it down—and not just on the back of an envelope. Keep a special journal for information related to your legal affairs and be sure to date the entries.

• *Maintain a schedule.* If your lawyer gives you a tentative schedule of the steps he plans to take on your behalf, write the schedule down. Review it from time to time. If your case seems to be falling behind schedule, call your lawyer and ask for an explanation and a revised schedule.

• *File it away.* Maintain a file of the information you have written down as well as your copies of legal documents and other papers related to your legal affairs. Conscientious file-keeping pays off in the preparation of a case, in trial testimony, in appeals, and, if necessary, in any subsequent action you may take against your lawyer.

Some Knowledge of the Law

One reason many lawyers don't bother to keep clients informed about their cases is that the clients don't know enough about the relevant law to make the information meaningful: "I'd like to spend more time explaining things to my clients," says an attorney in Chicago, "but it takes a lot of wasted time—and they never really understand anyway."

Of course, lawyers are largely to blame. If laws were written in plain English, or at least written about in plain English, it would be a lot easier for laymen to understand them. Sanford Kadish, Dean of the University of California at Berkeley Law School, says lawyers are masters of "a mysterious art form to which the layman is not privy, with mumbo-jumbo going on."

If you have a legal problem, do a little homework. No matter how good your lawyer is, some knowledge of the law will make your questions more informed and his answers more intelligible. Besides, you really can't be sure your lawyer *is* good unless you yourself know something about the law.

• *Don't be intimidated by jargon.* If you're particularly dedicated, you can spend time in a law library with a legal thesaurus or dictionary of legal terms in order to "translate" the key documents in your case. Jargon is still the cancer of legal writing, although in recent years many legal writers and even some lawyers have tried to reduce the "jargon quotient" and bring clarity to their written material.

• *Ask your lawyer.* There is hardly a subject in the law that hasn't been explained, in some form, in a popular book or magazine article. Your lawyer is the first resource for these kinds of materials, although he's more likely to know the professional books than the popular ones.

• *Ask a librarian.* If your lawyer can't help, the second resource is your local library. A law library is better for certain reference works, but if you're looking for an explanation of the law in plain English, a public or school library will probably be more useful.

Knowing When to Leave a Lawyer Alone

Just as you should offer to assist your lawyer when you think it might be helpful, you should keep out of his way when the assistance will be more of a hindrance than a help. Marvin Mitchelson, the famous California divorce lawyer, says: "A lot of people like to run their own lawsuits, especially in divorce suits. They like to get even, get retribution, score a point or two. You must learn how to check your own emotions." The failure to exercise self-control can interfere both with the success of your case and with the amicability of the lawyer-client relationship.

Not Expecting the Impossible

Your lawyer is obliged to provide reliable, thorough, prompt, competent, and reasonably priced legal services; he is *not* obliged to work miracles, or even to give you total satisfaction. Being realistic about results is often the hardest part of a client's job. If the law is clearly against you, you can't expect your lawyer to win the case; if your adversary holds all the bargaining chips, you can't expect to negotiate a fat settlement. You shouldn't be happy with anything less than first-rate legal service; but you *should* be happy with that, even if the result is less than you had hoped for.

THE CLIENT AND THE LAWYER'S STAFF

In all but the smallest firms, it's common for a lawyer to hand some aspects of your legal affairs over to someone else in the firm, usually a younger associate who is less experienced and, therefore, less expensive. This is both accepted and acceptable practice as long as you see to it that certain conditions are met.

• *Make sure you know the junior employees.* If a junior employee is going to take a substantial part in handling your legal affairs, you should get to know him. That may require some effort, since most of your appointments will be with the senior lawyer. The effort is well worth it, however: Lawyers, like most people, tend to work harder and better for people they know and like.

• *Make sure the junior employees have the necessary skills.* It's acceptable for a junior employee to deal with the less complicated aspects of your legal affairs, but he should never be expected—or allowed—to handle problems that require the senior attorney's experience and expertise. A good lawyer knows which details can be left to subordinates without jeopardizing the client's legal interests.

• *Make sure the junior employees are adequately supervised.* A junior associate or paralegal should research your legal problems only if he is closely supervised by a lawyer with the experience to know what should be researched and, equally important, when additional research would not be productive. Adequate supervision of subordinates can save you significant amounts of money.

• *Make sure you pay less for the work of junior employees.* If a secretary does certain work, make sure you're not being billed at an associate's rate. Even some of the best law firms are known to play with billing rates. The primary advantage of allowing subordinates to do your legal work is cost savings.

• *Make sure junior employees are used whenever possible.* If you know the junior employees who are working on your case, if you're convinced that they have the necessary skills and are adequately supervised, and you've checked to be sure that their time is in fact being billed at a lower rate, then it's in your interest to urge your lawyer to have them undertake any aspect of your legal business that he thinks appropriate.

PERIODIC REEVALUATION

Never let more than three months go by without reevaluating your lawyer's services. Many things can happen over the course of a lawyer-client relationship that may seriously affect the quality of legal services being provided. Some serious personal problem may arise that makes it difficult for your lawyer to work as much or as well as before. He may take on a new and demanding client who diverts so much of his time and energy that your business is slighted. Here is a checklist of questions you should ask yourself periodically in reevaluating your lawyer's services:

- Does the lawyer seem well prepared?
- Is the lawyer doing what he said he would do in your initial interview?
- Does the lawyer still seem concerned about your affairs?
- Does the lawyer still handle the important aspects of your legal affairs himself?
- Has the case changed direction, and, if so, does the lawyer still have the necessary expertise to carry on?
- Is the lawyer keeping you adequately informed?
- Has the lawyer ever been less than candid with you?
- Is the lawyer charging you too much for the work he's doing?
- How has the lawyer compared with other lawyers you may have run into since he began working for you?
- Are you generally satisfied with the quality of the legal services rendered?

11.
FEE DISPUTES

A Chicago attorney wrote a six-page complaint, made several motions to delay his client's trial, then, thinking that a pending Supreme Court case might be favorable to his client, simply waited. He was right. The Court's decision was favorable and he won his case without even going to trial. When he submitted a bill for $41,725—834½ hours at $50 an hour—the shocked client disputed the fee in court and won. "To put the matter bluntly," said the judge, "we believe the claim is exaggerated probably on the order of eight times." In the end, the attorney received nothing.

The most common disputes between lawyers and clients are disputes over bills. Why? Clients will tell you it's because most lawyers overcharge if they think they can get away with it. Lawyers, of course, will tell you that clients who lose don't want to pay for losing and clients who win don't understand how expensive legal services are to provide. Whatever the reasons, the facts are clear enough: If you end up in a dispute with your lawyer, chances are it will be over his fees.

HOW TO PREVENT FEE DISPUTES

The best way to avoid fee disputes is to negotiate the fee agreement thoughtfully in advance and to put that agreement in writing (see Chapter 6). Careful planning is the best preventive medicine. Here are some rules to guide you in the fee agreement negotiations that should make any subsequent fee disputes unlikely:

- Discuss every aspect of the fee agreement in advance.
- Put the fee agreement in writing.
- Ask the lawyer to explain any word, phrase, or idea that you don't understand.
- If you are in doubt, take the agreement home for friends or associates to read.
- Don't sign any agreement until you understand it and are satisfied with all its terms.

WARNING SIGNS OF A FEE DISPUTE

No matter how carefully you prepare the fee agreement, there are times when disputes will arise. Lawyers, after all, are experts at reading contracts their own way. If you can't avoid fee disputes altogether, you can at least see them coming and prepare for them. Here are some of the common warning signs that should alert you to the possibility of a fee dispute somewhere along the line.

- *Inexperienced lawyer.* The problem with an inexperienced lawyer is that he's more likely to make a mistake in assessing the time and effort it will take to deal with your legal problem. If he does make a mistake he'll give you an inaccurate fee estimate. Experienced lawyers are more likely to catch the little details that can make the difference between a few hours and a few weeks of work.
- *Overanxious lawyer.* An overanxious lawyer is often, but not

always, also an inexperienced lawyer. The overanxious lawyer is so intent on getting your business that his vision of the case and the work it will require may be temporarily impaired. It doesn't really matter why he's anxious. It may be because he needs the work, or because he's interested in your kind of case. Whatever the reason, if a lawyer is *too* accommodating, too eager to please, make sure that you double-check his estimates by getting another lawyer's opinion.

• *Poorly drafted fee agreement.* If your fee agreement fails to take into account all of the likely outcomes of your case, you're asking for a fee dispute down the road. If, for example, you hire a lawyer on a contingency fee basis and fail to specify in the agreement a lower percentage fee if the case is settled, you may be stuck giving up a third of the settlement money to a lawyer who has done only a few hours of work on your case. "An ounce of fee agreement," cautions a Los Angeles attorney, "is worth a pound of fee disputes."

• *Client's lack of fee information.* If you don't know what a contingency fee is or how it works, you can do two things: Hope that your attorney will make you aware of the various problems with contingency fees before you sign an agreement, or hope that nothing unexpected will happen in the course of your legal battle. The more likely possibility is that you'll end up in a fee dispute which you'll lose. Ignorance is no excuse for a fee agreement that doesn't protect your interests.

• *Client's feelings of embarrassment.* Many clients are embarrassed to talk about fees. They believe bargaining is for flea markets and that it somehow insults the professionalism of attorneys. If you feel this way, you should keep in mind that a fee agreement is really an opportunity to plan, not to haggle. Most disputes over legal fees arise from surprises. The fee agreement, if carefully prepared, should minimize the possibility of surprise.

• *Client's belief in lack of control.* The client who doesn't believe he has any control over legal fees is the client who throws his hands up in the air every time the subject comes up, saying something like: "You're the lawyer; you tell me." We say again, treat legal fees as you would treat gardener fees, plumber fees, or any other fees. The only difference is that lawyers are nonunion and therefore must negotiate their prices. If you fail to negotiate up front, you may find yourself complaining at the other end.

WHEN YOU SHOULD DISPUTE YOUR LAWYER'S FEE

Even if you follow all the preventive measures carefully, even if you negotiate every aspect of the fee agreement in detail and put the results down in writing, a fee dispute can still arise. Don't think that just because you've negotiated a fee, you're stuck with it. If the lawyer does what he agrees to do, and charges you a reasonable price for doing it, the possibility of a dispute is remote. But there are a number of things which a lawyer can do *after* the fee agreement has been signed that will justify your refusing to pay the fee you agreed to.

As a general rule, you should dispute your lawyer's fee (in most cases, that will mean not paying them) in the following circumstances, *whether or not you have a signed fee agreement:*

- when you think the fee charged is excessive;
- when you think your lawyer hasn't done a good job;
- when you've paid the fee but you think your lawyer hasn't earned it;
- when you think your lawyer is guilty of misconduct.

The last of these, refusing to pay your lawyer's fee when you believe he's acted improperly, is covered in Chapter 14. In that case, your refusal to pay is really a part of your general complaint about misconduct. We will discuss each of the other three kinds of fee disputes in this chapter.

Excessive Fees

How does the legal profession define an "excessive fee"? According to the Canons of Ethics, a fee is excessive when a lawyer of "ordinary prudence" has reviewed the facts and is left with a firm conviction that the fee is indeed excessive. Not very helpful or reassuring. This is a difficult standard to apply, and therefore not applied very often. If you were a lawyer reviewing another lawyer's fees, wouldn't you be reluctant to label them excessive? That, of course, is exactly what happens most of the time. The fee arbitration boards set up by most bar associations are notoriously deaf to complaints filed by clients about lawyers' "excessive" fees.

In Pittsburgh, for example, a wealthy client filed a complaint against her lawyer because he charged her $10,000 plus costs for a simple, uncontested divorce which, if she'd gone to a legal clinic, would have cost between $50 and $100. After listening to both sides of the case, the local fee arbitration committee determined that "the client undoubtedly received many benefits from the experience and knowledge of the lawyer which were not billed directly but which were an integral part of the service rendered and for which the lawyer deserves compensation."

With that kind of double-talk to contend with, you may wonder if disputing a bill is ever successful. The answer, surprisingly, is yes. More and more, fees—especially court-awarded fees—are being carefully examined, and even over-turned. So far, at least, it has been judges, not other practicing attorneys, who have been willing to condemn excessive fees. One lawyer whose six-figure fee request was rejected by a court suggested that judges were being harsh "because fees like this aren't available to judges. I think they're jealous."

How does the average client know when a fee is excessive? There's no easy answer. A fee that gives you a financial heart attack is not necessarily "excessive"—although such a reaction is certainly an indication of a very high fee. Most experts, and some lawyers, agree that if, after thinking about it hard and honestly, you are firmly convinced that the fee is excessive, it probably is. "The *rule*," says one Boston attorney, "is excessive fees, if by excessive you mean disproportionate to the amount of work involved. The trick is that most fees are not *too* excessive. They're just a little excessive so that clients can never be too sure they're excessive or work up too much outrage."

The conclusion: *A lawyer's fee is excessive if you're strongly convinced that it is in light of the work he has done on your case—even after he has explained in detail all the services he has performed.*

To help you recognize an excessive fee more confidently when you see one, we've included below a brief description of the most common types of excessive fees: unsubstantiated fees, inflated fees, and unauthorized fees.

• *Unsubstantiated fees.* Sometimes a lawyer will charge you for a number of hours of work with no indication as to how the hours were spent, or without an adequate description of the nature of the work done during those hours. In either case, you should dispute the bill. Often, these hours are left unsubstantiated in order to cover up the fact that the work was done by secretaries or paralegals but is being billed at the lawyer's rate.

• *Inflated fees.* Short of outright lying (something most lawyers prefer to avoid), a lawyer can inflate his fees in two basic ways: He can do unnecessary work in order to charge you for more time, or he can charge you for his time at an excessively high rate. The first is difficult to detect; the second can be avoided by specifying the rate in the fee agreement.

• *Unauthorized fees.* A lawyer can undertake work that is outside the charge which you've given him. If, for example, you ask him to review a contract, he may take it upon himself to rewrite it from scratch. The fee for the latter is substantially higher than the fee for the former. If you're specific enough about the lawyer's services in your fee agreement, however, you won't be obligated to pay for any additional work the lawyer undertakes on his own initiative.

Work Not Worth the Requested Fee

This is probably the most common kind of fee dispute. It is often mistaken for a dispute over excessive fees, but is, in fact, something very different. The immediate question here is not the quantity of work that was done, or the price charged for it, but the quality of it. If the lawyer had done the work well, the fee wouldn't be in question; it wouldn't be considered "excessive." (Of course, it's possible to have a fee request which is *both* excessive and "inappropriate" for substandard work.)

Typically, the client loses his case and then withholds payment of his lawyer's fee because he feels the lawyer bungled it. There are cases in which you can justify this course of action, but only under certain conditions:

- You think the lawyer lost the case because he didn't give it proper attention.
- You think he lost the case because his handling of it was incompetent.
- You think there was some dishonesty involved in his handling of the case (e.g., a conflict of interest).

This is a difficult situation because many clients who have bad cases or weak cases tend to put the blame on their lawyers; when they lose, it's considered the lawyer's fault. It's the old story of blaming the messenger for the message. How do you distinguish between a weak case (a case that even Clarence Darrow couldn't win) and a weak lawyer?

The first step, as always, is to talk with the lawyer. Ask him to explain his actions, or his lack of actions. If you're not satisfied with his explanation, consult other attorneys. This is rarely helpful—attorneys hate to second-guess each other—but occasionally you'll find one who's willing to give you a candid "second opinion." You might also consider asking a law professor for his advice. "We hear a lot of complaints," says

Professor Diane Acker of Washburn University Law School in Topeka, "and we're unbiased."

If you're still not satisfied, take your doubts to the local and state bar associations. They're not the most impartial groups around, but most of them do take their policing function seriously. If your lawyer's behavior was seriously inappropriate—and if he didn't merely show questionable judgment—they might take some action. You probably won't think it's enough, but it's also probably the best you'll get. (See Chapter 13, Disciplinary Action.)

Unearned Prepaid Fees

Disputes often arise when the client has prepaid some or all of his lawyer's fee and subsequently decides that the lawyer hasn't done enough work to earn that fee.

The best way to avoid disputes of this kind is not to pay your lawyer in advance. It's much easier for you to withhold money from your attorney than it is to get it back after you've given it to him. So, whenever you have a choice (and you almost always do), pay your lawyer as little as possible up front. If he isn't willing to provide all of his services before rendering a bill, try to break your case down into stages and pay him after the satisfactory completion of each stage. Remember, an unpaid fee is one of the few means at your disposal to insure that the lawyer does his job and does it well.

A Final Note: Your Lawyer's Reputation

You should avoid the natural tendency to think that overcharging is the exclusive weakness of small-time storefront lawyers trying to make a fast buck. In fact, one of the law firms caught most often with its hand in the cookie jar is Boston's redoubtable old firm, Hale & Dorr, the firm which includes Richard Nixon's former advocate, James St. Clair.

Hale & Dorr has twice been accused of overcharging on a

grand scale. In March 1981, a federal judge slashed the firm's $210,000 fee request in one case down to $50,000. The judge also deducted from the $50,000 an amount he claimed that Hale & Dorr had previously overcharged in the same case. In fact, it was the firm's request for a supplement to this first payment that triggered the judge's closer scrutiny of the $210,000 request. He likened Hale & Dorr's application for additional fees to "the thirteenth stroke of a clock, which raises serious doubts as to the reliability of the first twelve strokes."

So just because your lawyer, or his firm, rates a name on the door, don't be so sure you're getting what you pay for.

HOW TO CHALLENGE YOUR LAWYER'S FEE

The most important part of challenging a lawyer's bill is maintaining the right *attitude*. You should fight the tendency to think that it's somehow improper or unseemly to dispute the figure your lawyer submits. "Most clients consider challenging a bill unsportsmanlike, or something like that," says a prominent Los Angeles attorney who admits to being involved in numerous fee disputes, "And the reason they do is that most *lawyers* consider it unsportsmanlike." A young Boston attorney notes that "Lawyers are like doctors—they prefer it if the patient just lies there still and doesn't ask any questions."

When it comes to fees, however, what your lawyer prefers is irrelevant. It's your money and you're well within your rights not to pay a fee until you're satisfied that your lawyer has earned it. This is the first important lesson of fee disputes: *Don't be defensive about challenging a bill. It's not taboo to question a fee, even if that fee is in accord with the fee agreement.*

Once you've got the right mind-set, here are the procedural steps you should follow:

• *Review the bill.* Carefully look the bill over and make a note of the charges that seem excessive to you.

• *Request a meeting.* A telephone conversation will not suffice;

make it a face-to-face meeting. This will impress on the lawyer how concerned you are about it.

• *Have a full and frank discussion of the charges.* Don't pull any punches. You should ask the lawyer to describe *in detail* the work he's done on your case. (Incidentally, the lawyer should *not* charge you for the time spent at this conference.)

• *Negotiate.* Ask the lawyer to reduce the fee to a level which you think is appropriate. Be flexible and willing to pay slightly more than you otherwise would want to. A settlement now will save you the cost of prolonging the dispute.

• *Request a corrected bill.* If you and the lawyer reach a compromise solution you're satisfied with, ask him to resubmit the bill in a corrected version.

• *Consult friends and associates.* If you're not satisfied with the corrected bill, consult with people you know to see if they agree with you about the unreasonableness of the charges in question. This is especially helpful if you have a friend who is also a lawyer.

• *Go back to your lawyer.* If, after consulting with friends, you still think the charges are excessive, *do not pay them.* Go back to your lawyer and tell him that if you can't resolve the dispute, you will discharge him and find a replacement. This tactic often results in a compromise since the lawyer knows that it's much more difficult to collect *any* money from a non-client than from a client.

• *Consult a more senior partner.* If the lawyer himself is unresponsive, and he's not a senior partner in his firm, you might consider bringing the matter to the attention of a more senior partner. The senior partner may simply side with his colleague, or he may try to mediate the dispute.

• *Retain a new lawyer.* If your lawyer rebuffs this second effort to arrive at a compromise, *replace him.* Consult with the new lawyer both on your original legal matter and on the matter of resolving the disputed fee with your previous lawyer.

• *Take the dispute to the local or state bar association.* Many of these have established special procedures for handling disputes over fees which normally involve arbitration of some sort (see the section below on fee arbitration boards). Before taking this step, you should inform your original lawyer of your intentions and give him another opportunity to compromise.

• *Withhold payment and respond in court.* If the arbitration process is not satisfactory (if you're ordered to pay the excessive charges), you may still have the option of not paying, in which case the original lawyer may go to court to force you to pay. This is a new job for your new lawyer.

At various points in this process, you'll certainly want to weigh the costs of fighting over the disputed fee against the cost of going ahead and paying it. The amount of money in dispute and your chances of prevailing will be the two primary factors in your decision. You may decide it's not worth paying one lawyer to help you avoid paying another.

FEE ARBITRATION BOARDS

Most state and local bar associations have established fee arbitration boards to hear disputes over fees between clients and lawyers. The odds of getting satisfaction from one of these boards are not favorable. Most are made up exclusively of lawyers, meet in private, and pit you against your lawyer before a panel of his peers. To make matters worse, you often can't merely "test" your case in front of one of these boards. In most states, both parties must agree in advance to be bound by the decision of the board. Usually there is no appeal if you don't get satisfaction.

Obviously, your attorney will probably prefer to take the dispute to a fee arbitration board. In a court, he would have to argue in front of a jury of *your* peers, the hearing would not be closed, and the outcome would become part of the public record.

For all these reasons, you should consider the threat of going to trial a significant bargaining chip. Your attorney's desire to avoid public trial might be your best ally in winning a satisfactory settlement before having to take your case anywhere. Of course, if the lawyer calls your bluff and you end up in court, the process will cost you more and will take more time than an arbitration board hearing, but your chances of winning will be much improved.

Tips on the Arbitration Hearing

If you do decide to submit your complaint to a fee arbitration board, keep the following tips in mind:

- Try to find a board that includes nonlawyers (check both the state and local associations).
- Don't expect miracles. You're better off arguing for a reduced fee than for no fee. You'll look less like someone just trying to avoid paying for something he's already received.
- Try not to agree to be bound by the board's decision beforehand. Some boards will require that you sign an agreement to this effect. If you can, find a board that has no such requirement. That way, if you're dissatisfied with the result, you can take your complaint to court.
- Document your case as best you can. Here is where the records you have kept and the diary of your conversations with your lawyer will be very helpful.
- If the dispute involves a great deal of money, it's probably worth your while to contact another lawyer to help you prepare your argument before the board.

After Arbitration, What?

If your lawyer doesn't agree to submit the fee dispute to arbitration (an unlikely event), or if the board rules against him and he refuses to follow the board's decision, you'll probably have to take him to court. And the problem of finding a lawyer to take your case against the first lawyer will appear all over again.

What happens if you wait and instead of taking the dispute to either an arbitration board or court, you simply don't pay the attorney's bills and wait for him to do something? What are *his* options?

He can try to collect the bill on his own. Usually, attorneys do not collect their own bills; they hire other attorneys to do the dirty work. He can—but rarely does—go to a collection agency. Or he can take you to court. As a general rule, however, lawyers rarely take clients to court to collect unpaid fees, especially if the amount involved is small. Why? Because it's considered unseemly and detrimental to the lawyer's reputation. It's just not proper for a lawyer to sue a former client. Such a lawsuit could jeopardize the confidentiality of the attorney-client relationship and make the lawyer's current clients nervous.

WHAT HAPPENS WHEN YOU CAN'T PAY?

What do you do when the fees are not "excessive" by anybody's standards including your own, but you still can't pay them? What do you do when that awful moment arrives: A bill comes and you just can't pay it? Here are your options and the risks each one carries with it:

- You can tell your lawyer to stop doing work on your behalf. Suspending work, however, especially if your case is at a crucial stage, can seriously damage your legal interests and probably your chances of winning your case.
- You can renegotiate the fee agreement. Renegotiating a lower fee could remove some of the lawyer's incentive to do a thorough job. It's also very difficult to persuade a lawyer to reduce a negotiated fee.

- You can look for another lawyer who will charge you less. Changing lawyers, however, has its own set of risks, and there's always the possibility that the extra time which the second lawyer needs to "catch up" will end up costing you more than you would have paid if you'd stayed with the original lawyer.
- You can tell your lawyer to do less, or to do only certain limited tasks. Asking a lawyer to reduce his level of activity, however, increases the risk that he'll provide inadequate legal service and your interests will be adversely affected.
- You can try to settle the case quickly. Any effort to settle under financial pressure, however, is bound to result in an unfavorable—or at least less favorable—settlement.

Can You Discharge a Lawyer to Whom You Owe Money?

Yes. Many lawyers think that if you owe them money, they can refuse to withdraw from a case when you ask them to do so. In fact, no such right exists under the Code of Professional Responsibility. In most states, a client has an absolute right to discharge an attorney at any time and for any reason, no matter how much money is owed in unpaid fees (see Chapter 12).

The attorney, however, can *voluntarily* withdraw from the case if you owe him fees as long as he doesn't prejudice your legal interests by doing so *and* as long as he gives you due notice of his withdrawal. Even if you deliberately disregard an agreement or obligation to pay your lawyer's fees, he may not withdraw if by doing so he would prejudice your rights.

What can a lawyer do if you fire him while you still owe him fees? One of two things: He can keep whatever money or property of yours that he already has (as long as you didn't give it to him for a specific purpose), or he can wait and take his fees out of any money compensation that comes out of the case on which he was working.

12.
DISCHARGING YOUR LAWYER: WHEN TO CUT YOUR LOSSES

Fee disputes are the most common kind of lawyer-client disputes, but they're not the only kind. Yours would be a rare relationship indeed if you never disagreed or argued with your lawyer. That doesn't mean that you don't like and respect each other, or that the relationship should be terminated. Good lawyer-client "marriages"—like good husband-wife marriages—can weather disagreements and even an occasional falling-out. If there is mutual respect, the relationship can even be enriched by regular, friendly squabbling.

But there are other times when it's apparent to both of you that something is fundamentally wrong. It may be the lawyer's fault (something he said or did, or didn't say or do), it may be your fault, or it may just be a basic incompatibility. Whatever the reason, if the relationship isn't working well, it will usually be up to you to end it.

This chapter is about discharging your lawyer. It is, undoubtedly, an unpleasant task which most clients earnestly try to avoid—even to their own detriment. Yet it's a task which you should be willing to undertake if the circumstances demand it. This chapter will make the task easier by helping you to recognize when you should discharge your attorney and by showing you how to discharge him cleanly and fairly. In addition, you'll learn how to cope with the problems you'll face when you discharge your attorney, how to find a new lawyer to replace the one you've discharged, how to protect your right to competent legal services during the transition from one lawyer to the next, how to deal with the first lawyer after you've discharged him, and how to protect yourself from the first attorney's attempts at reprisal—if they come.

THE RIGHT TO DISCHARGE: FIRE AT WILL

You should have one thing very clear in your mind whenever you are considering discharging your lawyer: *Your right to discharge your lawyer is (nearly) absolute.* You can discharge your attorney at any time, for any reason, without any obligation (except by courtesy) to offer an explanation.

You'll hear this "absolute" right referred to over and over again by critics of the legal profession and even by lawyers themselves, but we feel obliged to add that it's not, in fact, *absolute*. There are a few extremely rare circumstances in which you can't discharge your lawyer. You can't, for example, discharge your attorney if you're doing so solely for the purpose of obstructing justice by causing an otherwise unjustifiable delay.

But this and several other minor exceptions aside, you can discharge your lawyer without cause: You don't like the way he talks, the suits he wears, the cigars he smokes, the color of his eyes. The reason doesn't matter. It doesn't even matter whether your agreement with him is written—as it should be—or verbal.

Even though all clients have this right, few exercise it. Why? Partly it's because people generally don't like to confront other people with their true feelings; it's just plain embarrassing. Too many clients suffer the disadvantages of substandard legal service simply because they can't bring themselves to dismiss their lawyers. This is especially true if the lawyer is a "nice guy," an old family friend, a pillar of the community, or a regular, reciprocal customer.

Another reason clients don't discharge their lawyers more often is that they're afraid of the consequences. Often, they don't know that their right to discharge is absolute and they fear the harm that could be done to their legal interests if they talk about a discharge that never takes place. Other common anxieties associated with discharging a lawyer are that:

- The lawyer knows too much and can use that knowledge to harm the client after being discharged.
- It will be difficult to find another attorney to replace the one discharged. Firing a lawyer can be a permanent stigma on a client in the professional community.
- The client will have to pay more than if he stays with the first attorney.
- The first attorney won't cooperate with his replacement—assuming one can be found.

All of these anxieties are discussed in this chapter and, in general, they amount to nothing. It's true, however, that the risk you run when you discharge your lawyer depends to a large extent on how you go about discharging him.

We don't mean to imply that changing lawyers is either safe or easy. For example, if you're in the middle of a case, changing lawyers can seriously disrupt the presentation of evidence, affect the jury and judge, and ultimately jeopardize your chances of prevailing. Even if you're not in court, discharging one lawyer and hiring another presents some major logistical problems: familiarizing the new lawyer with your affairs, moving documents and other materials from the old to the new lawyer's offices, arranging briefings between the old and new lawyers, establishing a working relationship with the new lawyer, etc. These are burdens that should not be assumed lightly.

For all of these reasons, we recommend the following two rules if you are contemplating discharging your lawyer:

Rule 1. When you're considering discharging your lawyer, observe the following procedure:

- Give your lawyer a chance to explain the actions which you consider a basis for discharge.
- Weigh the advantages of replacing your lawyer (better relationship, better representation, etc.) against the disadvantages of finding another one (time, expense, familiarization with your case, etc.).
- Contact other lawyers and nonlawyers to get a better sense of the generally accepted standards of behavior for lawyers in your area. This will allow you to judge more objectively the actions which you think justify discharge and to get other opinions.
- If you're still convinced, or even reasonably sure that discharging your lawyer is the best thing to do, do it.

Rule 2. Do not discharge your lawyer except for "good cause."

DISCHARGING YOUR LAWYER FOR GOOD CAUSE

If you discharge your lawyer for no reason, or no good reason, you'll have to pay him the reasonable value of the services he has rendered up to the time you discharge him. If, however, you discharge him for "good cause," *you don't have to pay him.* This is one of the great secrets of the legal profession.

In this context, "misconduct" does not mean a major offense; it doesn't have to be something criminal or even something that rates disciplinary action. It certainly doesn't have to be serious enough to warrant a malpractice suit or a criminal charge.

Actually, "misconduct" includes a lot of behavior that's relatively common in the legal profession—especially neglect. "I must admit," states an ABA official, "the rules about misconduct read differently than they play. If you took them seriously, I think a lot of lawyers would lose a lot of business. Fortunately, nobody seems to be taking them too seriously."

HOW CAN YOU RECOGNIZE MISCONDUCT?

An Iowa lawyer fell asleep several times during jury selection. Neither his client nor the judge would have known about it if the lawyer's glasses hadn't fallen into his lap in the middle of the proceedings. Several times, the judge had to order the bailiff to jostle the lawyer awake.

Some forms of misconduct, like sleeping through your client's case, are obvious. But misconduct does not have to be either obvious or criminal to be the basis for discharge. In some cases, it can be just an "innocent" mistake. A New York lawyer was cited for contempt of court, fined $2,500 and sentenced to fifteen days in jail for being two hours late to an assault trial. His client then dismissed him and properly refused to pay for his tardy services.

There are really two kinds of misconduct: One has to do with the way your lawyer handles your legal affairs, the other with the way he handles you. Either one is sufficient to get a lawyer discharged. Even if your lawyer does a good job handling your case, you're justified in replacing him if he doesn't treat you properly. By the same token (and much more common), no matter how well you and your lawyer get along, if he mishandles your legal affairs, you should seek a replacement.

Neglect

Neglect is far and away the most common form of lawyer misconduct. If allowed to go too far, it can be the basis of disciplinary action (see Chapter 13), or even a malpractice suit (see Chapter 14). Because neglect can have such serious consequences, you should be especially watchful for signs of it. If your lawyer begins to be neglectful in the little things, you should probably discharge him and look for another lawyer immediately, rather than wait until his neglect has seriously jeopardized your legal interests. Here are the warning signs to watch for:

- if he doesn't answer your phone calls or letters promptly and fully;
- if he puts you off when you ask important questions;
- if he fails to explain things to you;
- if he often gives excuses when you ask him if something has been done;
- if he holds hurried, abrupt office appointments;
- if he forgets your name or key facts about your case;
- if long periods go by when you don't hear from him and he does nothing on your case;
- if he refers all of your business, your calls, inquiries, etc., to underlings such as secretaries, junior associates, or paralegals.

What should you do if you feel your attorney is neglecting you? First, you should tell him. If the neglect continues, tell him that you're going to complain to the appropriate authorities (bar associations, etc.) if the neglect continues. Don't be vague about it. Tell him you plan to complain on a specific day if he doesn't shape up in the meantime. If the neglect still continues, file the complaint (see Chapter 13). This is one way you can strike a blow for better legal services. Also, be sure to tell him that if the neglect continues you'll dismiss him. If, after all this, the neglect persists, dismiss him.

If your lawyer has neglected your affairs, there's a good possibility he won't object to your taking your business elsewhere as long as you agree not to file a complaint. Few lawyers want the world to know that they've neglected a client's case. You can use this to your advantage. If, for example, you disagree over the amount of fee that's due, offer to refrain from filing a complaint if the lawyer will compromise on the fee.

Beware of the lawyer who offers to "let you" take your case to another attorney on the condition that you refrain from filing a complaint. As we've said repeatedly, you have an absolute right to leave your attorney at any time, for any reason. You don't need his permission to take your business elsewhere, and you certainly don't need to surrender your right to file a complaint. This sort of arrogant deception is itself grounds for a complaint to the local and state bar associations.

Incompetence

The major difficulty in discharging (or suing) a lawyer for incompetence is in recognizing it (see Chapter 14). Because you don't know anything about the law or the procedures involved, it's very difficult for you to know when your lawyer has made an outright mistake, much less an error in judgment. Even if you talk to other lawyers, you'll probably find them reluctant to second-guess one of their professional colleagues, much less suggest that the colleague may have acted incompetently. Bar association review boards—in some states, these boards are independent of the bar associations—are usually stacked against the client in a variety of ways (see Chapter 11).

So what can a client do if he has reason to believe that he's been the victim of incompetence? In general, follow the procedure we are about to outline, stopping only when all your questions have been answered and you're satisfied either that your lawyer was not, in fact, acting incompetently, or that you've been appropriately compensated and the lawyer has been appropriately penalized:

• *Talk to the lawyer.* Insist that he explain his actions and the reasons behind them in detail.

• *Consult a more senior partner in the firm.* Bear in mind, however, that such a person may or may not be willing to discuss the matter with you.

• *Consult other attorneys.* You may have to talk with several before getting a straight answer. Try an attorney in a nearby town if you suspect bias on the part of those in your own community.

• *Consult a law professor.* Some law professors consider themselves impartial in matters involving practicing attorneys.

• *Go to the state or local grievance committee.* Inform your lawyer of your intention to do this. (See Chapter 13.)

• *File a malpractice suit.* (See Chapter 14.)

Misconduct: A Checklist

We've listed below a number of common situations in which you have good reason to believe that your lawyer is guilty of misconduct:

- when your lawyer does nothing on a case for a long time or neglects your business in such a way that his inaction or neglect damages or jeopardizes your interests;
- when your lawyer fails to follow your instructions (as long as those instructions are legal and reasonable);
- when your lawyer fails to inform you of important developments in your case;
- when your lawyer fails to render competent legal advice;
- when your lawyer fails to maintain confidentiality;
- when your lawyer fails to supervise the people he directs to handle aspects of your case (this applies to secretaries as well as to associates and paralegals);

- when your lawyer violates the fiduciary relationship between you by failing to deal with you honestly and fairly;
- when your lawyer fails to perform the services he said he would perform in your agreement, whether written or verbal (this is often difficult to establish since most agreements are very vague on the question of exactly what services are to be rendered);
- when your lawyer commits an illegal act. The act must relate to your case or to your relationship with the lawyer. An unrelated illegal act probably won't constitute "good cause" and you won't be able to withhold compensation, unless that act impugns the attorney's honesty and integrity;
- when your lawyer commits an act, engages in behavior, or conducts himself in a manner that violates the Code of Professional Responsibility or other ethical code in your jurisdiction. This will often be hard for you to know unless there's been a determination by the grievance committee of the local bar association and even then because such decisions are rarely made public.

If you've talked with your lawyer and, where appropriate, with other lawyers, and you remain convinced of his misconduct, you'd be justified in dismissing him and refusing to pay any remaining fees. Depending on the circumstances, you might also be justified in taking further action, such as filing a complaint with the local and state grievance committees or instituting a malpractice suit.

Offensive Behavior

This kind of misconduct has nothing to do with your lawyer's handling of your case, but with his mishandling of *you*. Some examples of improper behavior:

- When your lawyer is discourteous or disrespectful. To justify dismissal or further disciplinary action, the behavior should be serious and unjustified, not minor discourtesies or lapses in decorum.
- When your lawyer takes a scornful, disparaging, or unconcerned attitude toward your legal interests. If you're getting a message from your lawyer that he just doesn't give a damn about your problems, or that your concerns are silly, you should begin to think not only about your relationship with him, but also about the effectiveness of his representation. Such behavior is certainly an indication that you need a new lawyer, and, if it's serious enough, it's probably a good sign that you should file a complaint.
- When your lawyer says or does something that seriously offends your sense of social, moral, or personal decency. Again, we're referring here to major offenses, not minor embarrassments. If you have special sensibilities in this regard, it's wise to advise your attorney of them at the start of the relationship. Otherwise, you have a right to expect acceptable social behavior from your lawyer at all times. If you do choose to discharge a lawyer for this reason, however, you should be aware that you might not be able to establish "good cause" and therefore might have to pay him compensation for the services he's rendered. What you consider seriously offensive, an arbitration board or court might not.

THE PROBLEMS OF DISCHARGING A LAWYER

Discharging a lawyer, even for good cause, is not without its problems. Generally, these problems fall into two categories: the problems of finding a new lawyer to replace the old one, and the problems of dealing with the old one so the discharge won't disrupt your legal affairs. Both kinds of problems tend to be less urgent if you've discharged your lawyer for misconduct.

Finding a New Lawyer

Discharging one lawyer will just create the need to replace him with another lawyer: a process that can be costly and time-consuming. The replacement lawyer will need time to familiarize himself with your case and, as you know, a lawyer's time is your money. There's also a possibility that the first lawyer will not want to or be able to share with his replacement all of his insights into your case, even though he's under a strict obligation to share all of his working papers.

If your lawyer withdraws—but probably not if you discharge him—he may want to associate you with another lawyer whom he knows or works with. He's not required to make this referral, but it's customary practice. However, under no circumstances are you required to accept the second attorney.

If you simply can't find a lawyer who'll handle your case—or the complaint against your first lawyer—the next best route is to contact the local bar association, the state bar association, or the grievance committee. They should be able to refer you to a lawyer who'll take on your case and, if necessary, help you prepare your complaint against the first lawyer and advise you on the chances of prevailing.

While you're looking for a replacement for the discharged lawyer, you will have to weather the transition period. During this time you should be concerned with:

- protecting your rights;
- finding a replacement;
- settling any outstanding fee disputes with the first attorney;
- obtaining any files, records, documents, etc., that are in the possession of the first attorney.

If your first attorney is relatively cooperative, these tasks shouldn't be difficult. If your parting wasn't amicable, however, the transition period can be difficult and, if protracted, can seriously jeopardize your legal interests.

Dealing With the Old Lawyer

Not surprisingly, the primary problem in dealing with the old lawyer centers around the question of money. If you pay him everything he says you owe him, you'll probably part ways amicably. If not, anything can happen.

Whether it's because you accuse him of misconduct, or simply because he says you owe him more than you think you do, if you *don't* pay your first lawyer, you can run into some serious problems. He can keep whatever money or papers or effects that you may have given him for safekeeping until you do pay him. That may not seem like much, but it includes all the papers relating to your case, the papers that your new attorney will need to see to do his job effectively.

Also, if you don't pay the first attorney, you may have special problems finding another attorney to replace him. Most attorneys won't agree to take a case unless and until you have been "released" by your original attorney. And no attorney is going to "release" you until you're paid up.

The most typical controversy occurs when you think you're dismissing your lawyer for good cause and therefore owe him nothing, but your lawyer disagrees and insists that you do owe him compensation for the services he's rendered up until dismissal. Often, the only way out of this confrontation, short of going before an arbitration committee or a court, is to compromise. If you're in the middle of changing lawyers, your affairs are going to be complicated enough without having to fight a peripheral lawsuit with your previous attorney. Besides, the first attorney can hold your papers and money, if he has any, for ransom.

A Lawyer's Obligation on Discharge

The discharged lawyer has an obligation, imposed by the Code of Professional Responsibility, to see that the discharge doesn't have any adverse effect on your legal interests. This means he can't hold papers for unreasonably long periods, or fail to notify you of important court-imposed deadlines. These obligations make the original attorney an important part of the transition period, during which your legal rights can be jeopardized by the lapse in representation. It's a good idea, therefore, to part with the original attorney as amicably as possible. Settle the compensation arrangements as quickly as possible—or at least appear to *want* to settle them. If, in fact, you can hardly wait to file a malpractice suit, at least wait until you have another attorney looking out for your interests before you turn and attack the one you left behind.

If the parting is not amicable, a discharged lawyer *can* make your life difficult—despite the Code of Professional Responsibility. In addition to holding your money and documents hostage, he can refuse to hand over his working papers, court documents, and other materials. The attorney is under an obligation to surrender these things upon dismissal, but there are a variety of stalling tactics which he can use to slow the transfer process and seriously impair the efforts of your new attorney.

He can also refuse to assist in familiarizing your new lawyer with your case. He may refuse to talk about the status of your case, about what he has or has not done, or, more urgently, what needs to be done immediately in order to represent you effectively. He may also refuse to recount to the new attorney the substance of conversations he's had with you or with other key participants in the case. These can be minor inconveniences, but if they come at a crucial time they can have a serious detrimental effect.

Discharging a Lawyer Employed on a Contingency Basis

The primary problem that arises when you discharge a lawyer whom you had planned to pay on a contingency basis is determining how much you owe him. The difficulty can be compounded if you haven't demanded from him all along an accurate accounting of time he's spent on your case. If he claims he's spent several hundred hours, how can you dispute it?

An alternative solution is to base the compensation on a percentage of any settlement offer the lawyer might have negotiated up to the point of discharge. To do this, of course, there has to have been a settlement offer *and* the lawyer has to have recommended that you accept it. If he didn't think it was a reasonable offer, you can't expect him to be happy with a percentage of it. If there's been no settlement offer that the lawyer advised you to accept, you'll probably have to pay him for "the reasonable value of the services he has rendered" at an hourly rate.

TIPS FOR DISCHARGING YOUR LAWYER

• *Talk with the lawyer*. It never hurts to be honest. Explain as fully as you can why you're considering dismissing him. Remember, you may have to rely on him during the transition period. There is always the possibility of a misunderstanding that can be cleared up relatively easily, and it's worth a try when you consider the difficulties and risks involved in changing lawyers.

• *Don't let the lawyer talk you out of it*. You may change your mind, but don't do so simply on the basis of the original attorney's urgings and assurances. Never drop your plans to dismiss a lawyer solely on the basis of what the lawyer says to you. *Always* consult at least one outside person, preferably another lawyer. It's true that lawyers tend to stick together, but that rule generally applies only in public. In the privacy of their offices, most attorneys are receptive and concerned about allegations of misconduct.

• *Don't let your doubts be ignored or downplayed.* When a lawyer hears that he's going to be discharged, he'll typically accuse the client of "overreacting." Or he'll imply that the problems are the *client's* fault. A lawyer who refuses to take your doubts seriously should be dismissed immediately.

• *Make arrangements for compensation.* If your discharge is for good cause, you shouldn't pay any compensation to the lawyer. If it's not for good cause, you should make some arrangements. More often than not, you'll think the discharge is for good cause, but the attorney will disagree; you'll think you don't owe him any compensation; he'll think you do. In this case, if you choose not to pay him, he may initiate proceedings against you.

• *Put everything in writing.* After you've talked with your lawyer, put everything you've said in writing: your reasons for discharging him and any arrangements you've made for compensation (or lack of it). Mail one copy, registered, to the lawyer and keep a copy yourself.

• *Make arrangements to have your files and other materials transferred to the new attorney.* Usually, you'll have to wait until the compensation arrangements are settled to do this.

• *Hire another lawyer to represent you.* You'll need another lawyer both to carry on the business that the first one began *and* to take care of any disputes with the first lawyer. Besides, if the first lawyer was really that bad, you probably need a lawyer all the more to straighten out your legal affairs and get your case back on track. It helps to let the replacement know that you fired the previous lawyer so that he understands clearly you won't tolerate substandard work.

• *Report the discharge to the appropriate authorities.* If you discharged your lawyer for good cause, you should report the dismissal to the local and state bar associations. This is true *whether or not* you intend to file a complaint with the bar associations. The letter should describe the reasons you discharged the lawyer and any damages you think you sustained because of the lawyer's misconduct. As always, keep a copy.

WHAT IF YOUR LAWYER WITHDRAWS?

There are two kinds of withdrawals: a voluntary withdrawal and a compulsory or mandatory withdrawal.

Voluntary Withdrawal

An attorney may choose to withdraw from a case, or from any relationship with a client, for a variety of reasons. The most common reasons for withdrawing are a client's lack of cooperation in preparing or presenting a case and failure to honor the fee agreement. There can be other reasons, of course, ranging from the attorney's case overload to failing health or just plain incompatibility.

There are important limitations on a lawyer's right to withdraw. The Code of Professional Responsibility states: "A decision by a lawyer to withdraw should be made only on the basis of compelling circumstances, and in a matter pending before a tribunal, he must comply with the rules of the tribunal regarding withdrawal." It goes on to say: "A lawyer should not withdraw without considering carefully and endeavoring to minimize the possible adverse effect on the rights of his client and the possibility of prejudice to his client as a result of his withdrawal."

In practice, this means that the attorney must observe a fairly standard procedure when he withdraws, a procedure designed to insure that his withdrawal does not adversely affect his client's rights:

- He must give due notice of his intention to withdraw.
- He must direct you to other counsel who will take his place (if you ask him to do so).
- He must deliver either to you or to the counsel you designate any papers or other materials he has relating to your legal business.
- He must cooperate with your new attorney.

- He must refund to you any compensation you've paid him which he hasn't earned (for example, a retainer that has been only partially spent).

Mandatory Withdrawal

There are several circumstances in which an attorney is *required* to withdraw from your case, even if you would prefer for him to continue to serve you. These are the most common circumstances:

- If your attorney knows or should know that you're suing somebody, conducting a defense, or pursuing something or somebody in the courts "merely for the purpose of harassing or maliciously injuring somebody." This rarely happens.
- If he knows or should know that by continuing to represent you he will be forced to violate the Code of Professional Responsibility or other disciplinary rules.
- If he knows or should know that a mental or physical condition makes it impossible or even unreasonably difficult for him to represent you effectively.
- If he knows or should know that continuing to represent you constitutes a conflict of interest.

13.
DISCIPLINARY ACTIONS

If you discharge your lawyer for good cause, you should file a complaint against him with the local and/or state bar associations. Of course, if his misconduct warrants it, you may also want to sue him for malpractice (see Chapter 14). But in almost every case of discharge for good cause, disciplinary action should be *automatic*.

We make this strong, risky, and unconventional recommendation for a variety of reasons. First, clients are the only ones who can effectively discipline lawyers. The bar associations have been claiming for years that lawyers can discipline themselves, but the studies and the statistics are to the contrary. The American Bar Association's own 1970 survey concluded that the state of legal discipline was "scandalous" and referred to the lawyer-run disciplinary system for lawyers as an "impoverished antique." If lawyers themselves don't have any faith in the system, why should clients?

Why, then, if the system is so shabby, do we recommend that you take part in it by filing a complaint? The answer is simple: If every client who has been the victim of a lawyer's misconduct files a complaint, the system will be overloaded to the point of collapse. Its inadequacy will become apparent, and, we hope, reform will become unavoidable. Filing complaints, whether or not they're adequately pursued, is the one way in which clients can bring pressure on the legal profession to clean up its own house.

There is another, less grand, and more practical reason for filing a complaint whenever you dismiss a lawyer for good cause. Remember that you have a right to withhold your lawyer's fee if you've discharged him for good cause. The fact that you've filed a complaint will give credence to your charge of misconduct and your refusal to pay the lawyer for his services. So by filing a complaint you can strike a blow for consumer protection and for personal economy at the same time.

This chapter will help you understand a little about how lawyers are disciplined (i.e., how they're *not* disciplined), how you can file a complaint, what the disciplinary process is like, what your chances of success in the process are, and what can happen to the lawyer if you're successful.

THE SORRY STATE OF LEGAL DISCIPLINE

The concept of an ethical lawyer has always been considered a contradiction in terms. For reasons too complex and debatable to go into here, lawyers have been the objects of public scorn and private mistrust at least since Shakespeare said, "first thing we do, let's kill all the lawyers." Their supposed lack of scruples or ethical standards is reflected in every survey of public opinion. In a recent Harris poll testing public confidence in various institutions, for example, the legal profession ranked almost at the bottom—below garbage collectors.

Some things are being done. In an effort to head off outside regulation, either from the government or from the courts, the national bar association and its state affiliates recently formulated some revisions of the old Code of Professional Responsibility that defines what is "ethical" and what isn't. These revisions call for more nonlawyers in attendance at disciplinary hearings, more public records, and a variety of other reforms designed to open up the disciplinary system and make it both more responsive to clients' needs and more effective.

The reaction of the legal community to these proposed changes is a good indication of how much most lawyers really want an effective disciplinary system. Samuel Siller, the president of the New York Criminal and Civil Court Bar Association, denounced the new provisions, saying they would open "a Pandora's box of evil consequences for the public and the accused." The proposed reforms have met with similar outrage from much of the legal community, demonstrating once again that many lawyers are in no mood to clean their own house.

How Lawyers Are (Not) Disciplined

In case you do have occasion to file a complaint against a lawyer with the disciplinary committee of a local or state bar association, you should have some idea of the ways these groups usually work. Although there are some variations in organization and procedures from state to state, they do have various characteristics in common.

Most lawyers are disciplined by other lawyers according to rules adopted by each state's highest court. The standards are then enforced either by a bar association group acting under a general authorization of the court, or by an independent group formed and supervised by the court.

Most complaints about these groups focus on two features: their composition and their procedures. Although some states have begun to put nonlawyers on disciplinary panels, they're still the exception rather than the rule. The fact that these groups are made up exclusively of lawyers not only casts doubt on their impartiality but also tends to intimidate prospective filers. One client who had discharged her attorney and considered filing a grievance complained, "What's the point? You'd have more luck complaining about Martin Bormann to a panel of Nazi generals."

Procedures are also a problem. They're numerous, onerous, and tend to favor the lawyer. In the past, according to Michael Franck, executive director of the state bar of Michigan, some states "provided more due process to a lawyer than to someone convicted of a capital crime."

Secrecy is a special procedural problem, not only because it keeps the public from knowing which lawyers have a record of misconduct (in most states it's illegal to give out any information about a complaint against a lawyer—even the fact that there is a complaint), but also because it keeps the grievance committee from knowing about a lawyer's record. As a result, lawyers with long histories of complaints are repeatedly let off as "first offenders" only because the committee has no record of the previous complaints.

The veil of secrecy extends even to disbarment, with the result that many lawyers who are disbarred in one jurisdiction can simply move to another to set up shop. There is now more sharing of information on disbarred and suspended lawyers than there used to be but abuses are still common.

Antiquated machinery isn't the only problem with the legal disciplinary system. Surprisingly, clients are also a problem. They simply don't complain. In fact, most experts agree that the main reason why lawyers get away with so much is that clients let them. Even when they discharge lawyers, most clients don't let anybody know about it. That's why we recommend that you should always notify the local and state bar associations when you discharge a lawyer for misconduct—even if you don't plan to press a complaint against the lawyer or file a malpractice suit.

FILING A COMPLAINT

Despite the fact that most clients are reluctant to do it, filing a complaint is a remarkably simple procedure. All that's involved is writing a letter to the appropriate bar associations or, in some states, the appropriate court-supervised independent disciplinary committee. You can find the names and addresses of the relevant organizations in the phone book, or by calling the local courthouse or any attorney's office.

The letter should include your name, the name of the lawyer, and the nature of your complaint (including a brief description of the misconduct which is the basis for your complaint). It doesn't have to be particularly elaborate or articulate. A simple, direct description will suffice. From that point on, the disciplinary group should tell you what to do next.

It's one of the weaknesses of the legal disciplinary system that there is very little sharing of information between different groups. Even within a state, the local bar association is often unaware of complaints filed with the state bar association.

To protect yourself and to protect other clients from similar misconduct, when you file complaints, you should file them with *all* of the relevant groups in the state: usually the local bar association, the state bar association, and the state lawyer review committee.

WHAT ARE YOUR CHANCES OF SUCCESS?

What are your chances of getting satisfaction in a grievance committee hearing? The available statistics are not encouraging. In Pennsylvania, of the nearly 10,000 complaints filed in five years between 1973 and 1978, only about 1 percent (120 cases) resulted in public punishment of the accused attorney. In Texas, where 8,500 complaints were filed against lawyers

between 1975 and 1977, there were only 77 cases of public
punishment—again, about 1 percent. In New York City in
1978, there were 2,700 complaints and only 20 public disciplinary actions.

To give you a better idea of what happens to these
complaints, here are the figures for New York City from April
through December 1977: number of complaints—approximately 1,900; number of complaints resulting in private
warnings—34; number of complaints resulting in suspension—
4; number of complaints resulting in resignation—2; number of
complaints resulting in disbarment—7; number of complaints
resulting in *no action*—approximately 1,850.

Why are the statistics so discouraging? Partly it's because of
the antiquated mechanisms we talked about earlier. There's no
doubt that the procedures of most grievance committees and the
dispositions of the committee members favor the lawyer over
the client. "Although almost all complaints handled come from
clients," reports James Miller on the workings of the New York
City Grievance Committee, "the committee shows a distinct
tendency to take the word of a lawyer over that of a client, even
when the lawyer's record contains a long list of previous
complaints."

Another reason for the poor record of these committees is
that their disciplinary efforts have tended to focus on the small,
marginal practitioner with few financial resources and no
political clout in the bar associations. An observer might
conclude that there is no unethical conduct in the large, well-
endowed firms. Yet even the scanty public records indicate that
there's a great deal of misconduct in these hallowed, paneled
halls; it just goes benignly undisciplined by the bar associations.
In fact, the only lawyers from large firms publicly disciplined
in recent years have been disbarred under statutes that require
automatic disbarment for certain offenses.

What's In a State?

Unfortunately, what satisfaction you can get from a disciplinary committee depends ultimately on what state you're in. That's right—where you live can make all the difference. For example, there are thirteen states that have established disciplinary committees that are completely independent of the local and state bar associations. If you're lucky enough to live in one of these states, you're more likely to get a satisfactory resolution of your claim if you take it to a grievance committee.

This is only one "test" of an effective disciplinary system. Here are a number of questions you should ask about your state's grievance committees in order to estimate your chances of success. Remember, we recommend that you file the complaint whether or not you think it has much chance of success. But the answers to these questions (which you can get just by calling the local bar association or the grievance committee itself) will tell you what kind of results to expect.

• *Is the grievance committee independent of the bar association?* Satisfaction is more likely if it is than if it isn't.

• *Are there nonlawyers on the panels?* The more nonlawyers there are, the more likely you'll be satisfied with the determination.

• *Are the disciplinary hearings open to the public?* Remember, secrecy is a major problem with the disciplinary system. The more open it is, the more accountable it is, and therefore the better it is.

• *What range of penalties are available to the committee?* A good committee will have a number of penalties available to it. You should ask about the frequency with which each penalty is imposed. If they can't come up with the figures immediately, their record-keeping is shoddy and suspect.

• *Is there a right of appeal?* Many committees will require you not to press your claim if the committee makes a determination. Don't agree to any such deal. If you're unhappy with the decision, you should be able to go to court, either in a formal appeals procedure or as a plaintiff in a malpractice case.

• *Is there a backlog of claims?* How long is it and how long is the waiting period? This is often a good index of the budget which is available for disciplinary activity. If there is a huge backlog, don't expect too much. On the other hand, a backlog may mean that the committee is very diligent and conscientious in its handling of complaints, so don't let a backlog scare you away either.

• *What is the committee's record: the ratio of complaints to disciplinary actions?* This is the real test. The ratio will always be lopsided, but it shouldn't be too lopsided. If the ratio of complaints to public dispositions is greater than 20:1, the committee is not doing its job. Again, if the group doesn't have these statistics immediately available, that in itself is reason to doubt its efficacy.

• *Who funds the committee and how well?* Is it independently funded or is it funded by the bar association? How well is it funded? (The Washington State Bar Association committee—considered one of the country's best—spends more than $50 per lawyer on discipline. That's at the high end of the range. New York City is at the low end, with about $20 per lawyer. A reliable disciplinary system should spend between $35 and $45 for every lawyer it's supposed to police. If your state association doesn't spend that much, or doesn't know how much it spends, don't count on getting a satisfactory result.)

WHAT HAPPENS IF YOU'RE SUCCESSFUL?

If yours is one of the rare complaints that results in a disciplinary action against a lawyer, the nature of the punishment will depend on a variety of factors, some obvious and appropriate (the grievousness of the misconduct, the lawyer's previous record, the damage done to your legal interests), some remote and inappropriate (the lawyer's background, his connections in the community, the reputation of his firm, the nature of the case).

Most bar grievance committees have a broad range of penalties at their command: anything from a letter of caution or a mild and private personal reprimand to an inquisitorial hearing before a panel of lawyers followed by public censure, suspension, or disbarment. In general, these are the common penalties:

• *Private reprimand.* Issued in the form of a letter of warning, this is the lightest punishment. Only the lawyer and the complaining client know of the lawyer's misconduct—which is, of course, just as the lawyer wants it.

• *Public reprimand.* No permanent damage is done except to the lawyer's professional reputation. Although the information on the reprimand is available to the public, it's hardly common knowledge.

• *Suspension.* The period of suspension can vary from just a few days to several years. A suspension can also be indefinite or contingent on the lawyer's demonstrating that he has "regained good moral character."

• *Disbarment.* This is the professional equivalent of capital punishment, with one difference: A lawyer who is disbarred can petition to be readmitted. This ultimate sanction is reserved for the most egregious misconduct and serious felonies.

Disbarment is extremely rare. For several years, the rate of disbarment has been about even at 200 per year, or about .035 percent of the nation's 575,000 lawyers. Because it's such a serious penalty, disbarment is rarely applied automatically, without the formality of a hearing at which the lawyer can present the arguments why he shouldn't have his livelihood taken from him. In some states, if the lawyer is convicted of a felony (e.g., perjury) he's automatically disbarred, but in most it's only if the lawyer is convicted of a felony that directly impugns his honesty and integrity. There are even some states where a lawyer can continue to practice after being convicted of a serious crime until disciplinary proceedings are brought— which can be never. In almost every state, the lawyer is allowed to practice until all appeals have been exhausted, which can mean that he's still accepting clients and appearing in court three or four years after conviction.

If there is no state law which "triggers" disbarment, the penalty is almost never imposed. "I can only think of two things that are guaranteed disbarment," says one New York City judge, "baby-stealing and matricide." The standard may not be that restrictive (although a New Jersey lawyer was disbarred for his involvement in a baby-selling scheme), but it is strict. For example, a California lawyer was disbarred after being convicted on eight counts of grand theft and four counts of forgery. In disbarring him, the California Supreme Court noted both the seriousness of the offenses and the fact that the lawyer's conduct involved "moral turpitude"—a catch phrase for disbarment proceedings.

But when it comes to disbarment, punishment is never a certainty. Another California lawyer who was found guilty of misappropriating his clients' funds was merely placed on a three-year suspension. In refusing to disbar him, the court cited both his clean record and some emotional strain that he'd been under.

The standards can also bend according to your lawyer's background, the reputation of his firm, and the amount of money involved. A distinguished New York attorney was spared disbarment despite having lied and withheld important documents in a multimillion dollar antitrust case. The attorney, a senior partner at one of New York's oldest and wealthiest firms, had blue-blooded credentials, including Phillips Exeter Academy, Harvard College, and Harvard Law School. In declining to disbar him, the court felt that he had suffered enough indignity by having to resign from his firm and endure "the consequent humiliation and disgrace." There was no indication in the court's opinion as to whether the attorney had been forced to resign from his yacht club.

The moral is painfully clear: Even if your lawyer has impeccable credentials, you can't be sure he won't get caught cheating. But you *can* be pretty sure he won't get punished.

14.
LEGAL MALPRACTICE: WHEN DISCHARGE AND DISCIPLINE ARE NOT ENOUGH

Sometimes representation is so poor it's malpractice. When your lawyer renders services that are so inadequate that you are seriously damaged as a result, discharge isn't enough. Discipline isn't enough. A malpractice suit is the only way to recover your losses and feel satisfied that the lawyer has been justly penalized for his misconduct.

As you can imagine, you will run into a variety of problems when you try to sue your lawyer. For example, how do you know you've been the victim of malpractice? Can you get an honest assessment of your lawyer's competence from another lawyer? If you decide you've been a victim, how can you find a lawyer who'll sue another lawyer? While eager to sue doctors and other professionals, most lawyers are loath to sue a "brother at the bar." They consider it bad form, or, more to the point, "professional fratricide."

This chapter will help you overcome these considerable hurdles. It will help you decide first if you should file a malpractice suit: Is discharge enough? Will a disciplinary hearing give you satisfaction? Are there other ways of being compensated for your loss? Second, if you decide you should sue, it will help you through the thicket of problems and procedures that surround a malpractice award. Beating a lawyer at his own game is difficult, but it has its own, very special rewards.

Most people are simply too intimidated by the idea of suing a lawyer and therefore do nothing to redress a grievance. We said there are many reasons not to sue for malpractice, but this isn't one of them. If you do nothing, not only will you have to bear the burden of your lawyer's incompetence, so will other clients after you. In this respect, a malpractice suit is a public service, like getting a drunk driver off the road.

MALPRACTICE: AN INFLATIONARY MARKET

Inflation has definitely struck the malpractice market. The number of malpractice suits has doubled in the last five years and is expected to double again in the next five. Premiums on malpractice insurance for lawyers have followed suit, rising as much as 400 percent annually.

Why this rising tide of malpractice litigation? "The overriding cause of the coming crisis in [malpractice] litigation," says journalist Robert Kroll, "is the abundance of legal malpractice itself. The lawyer population is as morally frail, venal, and imperfect as any other group of people. Errors creep in; and outright fraud and deceit become ever more prevalent as opportunities expand."

The public is also more aware than it used to be that malpractice suits are available as a way to "get back at" incompetent lawyers. Such suits are now the grist for banner headlines. Many heads turned, for example—both inside and outside the legal profession—when Doris Day sued her long-time lawyer, manager, and business partner and was eventually awarded $26 million. There was also quite a stir in the papers when Patty Hearst sued her flamboyant attorney, F. Lee Bailey, for the unsuccessful outcome of her case.

Although such suits are far from typical, they do serve to publicize the issue of malpractice. "Every time someone reads in the paper that a lawyer has been successfully sued," says a prominent Chicago lawyer who has been successfully sued, "there's a little voice inside that stands up and cheers. People love to see a lawyer lose in court. And you can bet that the next time they run into a problem with a lawyer, they'll be thinking about that malpractice suit and how much *they* would like to beat a lawyer at his own game. I'm not surprised that malpractice is snowballing."

Whatever the reasons, malpractice suits are now much more readily available to the disgruntled client than they used to be. Client organizations will tell you that's a good thing; lawyers, of course, will tell you it's not. In fact, it's good and bad: good because lawyers should be held accountable for the damage caused by their negligence or incompetence; bad because many more clients are now tempted to file malpractice suits without understanding the problems involved or adequately exploring other possibilities for recovery of damages.

If you are thinking about initiating a malpractice suit, consider the following questions:

- How do you know it's malpractice?
- How will you find a lawyer to take the case?
- Is it worth the time, effort, and expense involved?
- What are the alternatives?
- What are your chances of success?

MALPRACTICE: HOW TO KNOW IT WHEN YOU SEE IT

The first step, of course, is to decide if you've been the victim of malpractice. Not all mistakes are malpractice. In general, the kind of misconduct that warrants a malpractice suit is very much like the misconduct that warrants discharge or disciplinary proceedings, only worse. According to the Canons of Professional Ethics, a lawyer is guilty of malpractice when he fails to exercise the knowledge, skill, and ability ordinarily possessed and exercised by a competent lawyer; when he fails to handle a client's case with reasonable competence, diligence, and care; or when he fails to act honestly, fairly, and in good faith in all his dealings with the client.

Put more simply, a lawyer is guilty of malpractice when he's *incompetent, negligent,* or *dishonest.* But incompetence, negligence, and dishonesty are not enough, by themselves, to support a malpractice suit. Your lawyer can be any one of these things, or all three, and you can still lose a malpractice suit against him. In order to sue a lawyer *successfully* for malpractice, you also have to show that your legal interests—your claim, or your rights—were *damaged* by the lawyer's incompetence, negligence, or dishonesty: for example, you lost your case, you didn't receive as much money as you should have, you had to pay more money than you should have, or you were sent to prison when you shouldn't have been.

As you may have guessed, proving that your lawyer was incompetent, negligent, or dishonest is relatively easy. Proving that his incompetence, negligence, or dishonesty resulted in damage to you is not. You must show that if it hadn't been for the lawyer's misconduct, you would have won your case, received more money, lost less money, or not been convicted.

Unfortunately, it's hard to be sure that your case meets these requirements without the aid of a lawyer. You may not know, for example, what skills "well-informed lawyers of ordinary skill and capacity commonly possess." But it will help if, before you see an attorney about filing a malpractice suit, you think about these requirements and how the facts of your case fit them. You're more likely to find an attorney willing to help if you can convince him that all the essential elements of the case are in place.

Incompetence

There are two basic ways in which a lawyer can be incompetent. He can make an error of *fact* because he simply doesn't know the applicable law or procedure, or he can make an error of *judgment*. Obviously, errors of fact are far easier to prove than errors of judgment. For that reason, an error of judgment has to be gross and obvious for it to be considered malpractice. If your lawyer makes a decision which you think is wrong, but others think is right, chances are it won't support a malpractice suit.

Errors of fact, on the other hand, don't have to be gross or obvious, but they *do* have to have caused some damage to your legal interests. Lawyers can't be expected to know everything, but they can be and are expected to know when they don't know something and to seek appropriate advice from someone who does.

To sue a lawyer for malpractice, his "incompetence" doesn't have to be certifiably insane, just extraordinary. In fact, it's sufficient grounds for a malpractice suit if your lawyer fails to research a topic thoroughly enough. In one California case, the client asked her lawyer a question which he answered incorrectly. On the basis of his answer, she agreed to a property settlement that was considerably smaller than she otherwise could have received. The woman sued for malpractice and won a $100,000 judgment in the California Supreme Court.

There's an old adage in the legal profession that a lawyer is the only person for whom ignorance of the law *is* an excuse. Fortunately, that's no longer as true as it used to be. For example, in Maryland, a state law required a particular signature on a note when the note related to a real estate sale. The attorney for a buyer should have known that, but didn't. The buyer failed to get the signature and, as a result, lost $140,000 on the voided sale—a loss that the attorney eventually made good.

The same problem arises in all these cases: How does the

client know the attorney has acted incompetently, that he's failed to research a subject thoroughly, or isn't familiar with the applicable law? Unfortunately, in most cases, the client doesn't know he's the victim of incompetence until it's too late, and often not even then. "Most cases of incompetence are never detected," says a New York lawyer who handles legal malpractice cases. "The client never really knows why things didn't turn out the way he wanted. He may mutter about his lawyer, but he wouldn't think of suing. There's no doubt about it, lawyers get away with murder."

The general duty to be competent really breaks down into four specific duties. You should keep these in mind when you're trying to decide if you've been the victim of malpractice. A violation of any one of them is sufficient to support a malpractice suit:

• *Duty to know.* Your lawyer must know the plain and elementary principles of law commonly known by well-informed attorneys. Obviously, violations of this duty are hard to detect unless you yourself happen to be a well-informed attorney. If you suspect that your lawyer doesn't know what he should know, however, ask another lawyer. While most attorneys are loath to second-guess another lawyer's *judgment*, they are usually willing to question another lawyer's knowledge of the law.

• *Duty to research.* Your lawyer must discover those additional rules of law which, although not commonly known, may readily be found by standard research techniques. In other words, a lawyer should know when he doesn't know. "You'd be surprised how often lawyers try to bluff an answer," says the Chicago lawyer who lost a malpractice suit and now considers himself a "born-again" reformer of legal ethics. "Coming up with an answer that sounds good and stating it with confidence are highly valued talents in the legal profession. That's fine for negotiating, but it can wreck havoc on a client's case."

• *Duty to do a good job.* Your lawyer must undertake reasonable additional research in order to learn relevant legal principles even in unsettled areas of the law. This is the most controversial of these "duties" and there are many lawyers who would deny that it exists at all. Understandably, they don't want to be put in a position where they have to go beyond the easy, standard research patterns in order to make a case for their clients. If you plan to base a malpractice suit on this duty, you should request from your lawyer a full description of all the research he's done on your behalf. You should also keep in mind that the duty to do a good job is *not* the same thing as a duty to *win*.

• *Duty to make good decisions.* Your lawyer must base his decisions about how to conduct a case on an intelligent assessment of the problem. That's not to say, of course, that he has a duty to make the *right* decision. This is by far the hardest kind of malpractice case to make, despite the fact that it's what most clients complain about the loudest. If you disagree with a decision your lawyer has made, and you think the decision caused you to lose the case, or kept you from getting as much money as you deserved, or sent you to jail, then you should be thinking about a malpractice suit. Getting another attorney to disagree with the first lawyer's decision will be difficult. When it comes to judgment calls, lawyers are like umpires. There has to be a mistake of monumental proportions before they start to disagree among themselves.

These four duties add up to a rigorous standard for competence. Unfortunately, it's a standard that's not very rigorously enforced. Says an ABA official candidly, "The general attitude among lawyers is: Judge not, that ye be not judged."

Negligence

The most common form of legal malpractice is negligence: A lawyer simply neglects his duties to a client. And the most common form of negligence is the failure to meet deadlines. The law is filled with deadlines: not just statutes of limitations that bar suits after a certain period of time, but also time requirements on the filing of motions, the service of process (filing complaints and answers), and a variety of other activities, all of which can directly affect the outcome of a case. Failure to be aware of and meet these deadlines can cause a client to lose an otherwise valid claim. This is also the most serious form of malpractice.

Unlike incompetence, negligence is relatively easy to detect. You may not know that a particular courtroom error cost you a case, but you'll know if your case never gets to court because your lawyer let a deadline pass. In addition, damages are easier to prove when your lawyer has been negligent. Usually the damage will be in the form of missed opportunities, legal rights that were lost: the right to sue, the right to collect, etc. Money may also be lost as a result of losing a legal right, and that money will be the measure of the malpractice award.

Dishonesty

Incompetence is the most difficult kind of malpractice to detect and negligence is the most common. But the most *obvious* malpractice occurs when the lawyer actually cheats you or steals your property. Such shenanigans are usually given more refined names ("misappropriation" of the client's property or "embezzlement" of funds), but it amounts to theft and you should know it when you see it.

The most important thing to keep in mind if you're thinking about suing your lawyer for malpractice on the basis of dishonesty—or "intentional wrongs," as they're referred to in the profession—is that most malpractice insurance policies don't cover this kind of misconduct. Of course, that problem is really subordinate to a much larger problem you may run into: Most lawyers who are dishonest can't *get* malpractice insurance at all. As a rule, the lawyers who need the insurance the most can't get it, which means that the real victims are not the lawyers who can't insure themselves, but the unwary clients who come to them and don't bother to ask if they're insured.

Fortunately, most states have corrected this anomaly by establishing client security funds which reimburse clients who've been victimized by dishonest lawyers. If you think you've been victimized this way, you might consider applying to one of these funds, bringing disciplinary proceedings against the lawyer, and foregoing a malpractice suit altogether. If there's little or no chance of recovery (because the lawyer is insolvent and has no insurance), you might do just as well to avoid the time and expense of a suit and settle for reimbursement.

THE FOUR MOST COMMON KINDS OF MALPRACTICE

Although malpractice comes in an infinite variety of forms and shadings, there are basically four major types. Because they account for almost all malpractice suits, you should be especially on the lookout for them:

• *Failure to file.* By far the most common form of malpractice occurs when the lawyer neglects to file papers with the court within the statutory periods, thereby allowing the statute of limitations to lapse and leaving the client powerless to bring the case to court again.

• *Commingling of funds.* This occurs when you give the lawyer money to hold in trust or to put in an escrow account and, instead of setting aside the money in a separate account, the lawyer puts the money in the same account with his own funds and subsequently uses your money. If he does so knowingly, then it's intentional misconduct—in this case, fraud—and the most serious grounds for a malpractice suit. More often, the lawyer is just lazy or negligent—less grievous faults, perhaps, but no less cause for a malpractice suit.

• *Failure to research.* The most common example is the sloppy title searcher. If a lawyer doesn't do a thorough and competent job of searching a title (i.e., finding out what claims are outstanding on a piece of property), somewhere down the road the client /purchaser can find that he doesn't own the land he purchased and can't recover the purchase money. Failure to research is becoming a more common ground for malpractice because the things that a lawyer needs to know are becoming more numerous. No lawyer can be expected to know everything, but he can be expected to know when he should research a particular question.

• *Failure to exercise due care.* This kind of incompetence is related to failure to research but more often involves specialists who are supposed to bring their expertise to bear on a client's problems and, if they fail to do so, may be liable for the resulting damages. The most common example is the tax specialist who draws up a will or a trust agreement but, because he fails to exercise due care, makes mistakes that result in tax burdens that could have been avoided. Thus, sometimes a lawyer can be liable not just for incompetent work, but for work that is competent but not competent enough.

REFERRALS AND MALPRACTICE

A new and still relatively uncommon form of malpractice involves referrals: the age-old custom by which one lawyer refers you to another lawyer, either because he's too busy or because he lacks the necessary expertise. This custom has been a notorious boondoggle in which lawyers, without regard for the client's interests or the qualifications of the other lawyer, maintain *quid pro quo* relationships to supplement their incomes.

No longer. A New York woman involved in a car accident went to her usual lawyer; he referred her to another lawyer who specialized in personal injury litigation. The second lawyer eventually settled the case for $150,000 while the woman was out of the country and, after obtaining a release, took the money and ran. In the malpractice suit that followed, the court ruled that the *first* attorney had been negligent in referring the woman to the second attorney without checking his credentials.

The moral is clear: If one attorney refers you to another attorney who subsequently acts improperly, they *both* may be guilty of malpractice.

PROFESSIONAL FRATRICIDE: THE PROBLEM OF FINDING A MALPRACTICE LAWYER

A California woman wanted to sue her divorce lawyer because he advised her that she wasn't entitled to half her husband's military pension in a divorce settlement when, in fact, the substantial monthly payments were subject to California's community property law. When she tried to find a lawyer who would take her malpractice suit, the woman was refused again and again. The reason: The lawyer who gave her the bad advice was the president of the local bar association.

The hard truth is that it's extremely difficult to find a lawyer who'll handle a malpractice case against another lawyer. This is especially true if the lawyer you're trying to sue is prominent in the legal community, is from a prominent firm, or is active in local bar affairs. If your local legal community is small, you'll probably have to look in surrounding communities for a lawyer willing to handle your claim. Even lawyers who routinely handle malpractice suits against doctors or other professionals are typically loath to "turn on their own" and press a malpractice suit against a fellow lawyer. Some lawyers think that lawyers who push malpractice suits are committing "professional fratricide." Others disparage them as the dregs of the legal community: hangers-on who can't find decent work. The vast majority simply consider legal malpractice suits in bad taste.

Part of the problem is with the clients themselves. Many people are uncomfortable with the idea of going to one lawyer to sue another lawyer. "There's a reluctance to approach the bar [with these kinds of problems]," says Sandy DeMent, executive director of the National Resource Center for Consumers of Legal Services. "It's like the hen going to the fox to complain about the hen house."

Because so few lawyers will undertake a malpractice suit against another lawyer, when you find one who will, he's likely to be a loner, a newcomer, or a professional pariah. "I don't belong to any clubs," says California malpractice lawyer Edward Freidberg, "I may be snubbed all over by lawyers because I sue other lawyers, but I wouldn't know it."

Of course, there are attorneys who are active members of their local professional communities, but nonetheless feel an ethical obligation to take a malpractice case now and then. "One of the attributes of the profession is fighting all day and enjoying a beer with your adversary in the evening," says Seattle attorney William H. Gates. "That does affect one's willingness to be involved in malpractice cases. It's darned unfriendly to sue or to testify as an expert witness, but it is an attorney's responsibility."

It's easier to find malpractice lawyers in major cities where the professional community is larger and less integrated. Wherever you live, however, there are various places you can go to find a malpractice lawyer, none of them entirely satisfactory:

- local and state bar associations;
- referral services;
- bar association grievance committees or committees on professional responsibility or discipline;
- state boards of bar overseers;
- lawyers in your area who handle other kinds of malpractice cases (especially medical malpractice).

If these fail, try going down the same list of possibilities in a nearby city and make it clear that your claim is against a lawyer who's not local.

TO SUE OR NOT TO SUE; THAT IS THE QUESTION

We said earlier that there are three questions you should keep in mind when you're considering suing your lawyer for malpractice: Are you sure it's malpractice? How will you find a lawyer to press your claim? How time-consuming and expensive will it be and, given the time and expense, will it be worth it? The last of these questions may, in fact, be the most important.

Let's assume you're *convinced* that your lawyer has been incompetent, negligent, or dishonest (or some combination of the three). Let's also assume that you can show that your lawyer's incompetence, negligence, or dishonesty resulted in damage to you. Let's even assume that you've talked with another lawyer, he agrees that you've probably been the victim of malpractice, and he's willing to take the case if you decide to press it. Does all this mean that you should sue?

Not necessarily. Just because you *can* file a malpractice suit doesn't mean that you *should*. That may be hard to accept if you've been victimized by a lawyer and you're convinced you can extract the revenge you so richly deserve. There's a very special pleasure in beating a lawyer at his own game. But there are also very good reasons to stop and think about the following alternatives before pressing a malpractice claim.

Convince Your Lawyer to Pay for the Damage

This is the best thing to do. You avoid the hassles and expense of a lawsuit, the lawyer avoids the embarrassment of a malpractice suit, even an unsuccessful one, and you are compensated for your loss. Unfortunately, this is also the least likely alternative. Unless the damage to you has been both undeniable and slight, your lawyer will probably deny any responsibility. There are exceptions to the rule, however, which is why you should *always* go to your lawyer and discuss your complaint before filing a malpractice suit. For example, if a lawyer has missed a filing deadline, thereby preventing you from recovering a debt, he is very likely to reimburse you. If, however, he's missed a deadline for suing for personal injury, there's only the remotest possibility that he can or will pay you the money that the jury would have. For that, you'll probably have to take him to court.

Take Your Complaint to a Bar Association Grievance Committee

The important distinction between a malpractice suit and a disciplinary action is that the purpose of a malpractice suit is to recover money from your lawyer to make up for the damage which his misconduct did to your legal interests, while the purpose of disciplinary action is to bring the lawyer before the appropriate authorities and punish him for his misconduct. In the latter, the punishment meted out is designed to discourage him from similar conduct in the future and to protect others.

The malpractice suit is supposed to *compensate* the client, the disciplinary hearing is supposed to *punish* the lawyer. Both functions are important, and both processes are designed to protect important interests. Therefore, if you've been seriously wronged, it's likely that you'll want to proceed with both. As a general rule, if you've been *damaged* by your lawyer's misconduct, a complaint before a grievance committee isn't enough. Also as a general rule, you probably should file a complaint with a grievance committee *whenever* you sue a lawyer for malpractice.

Seek Compensation from a Client Security Fund

The lawyers most likely to commit malpractice are the same ones who are least likely to have malpractice insurance. They're also not likely to have enough assets for you to satisfy any judgment you might secure against them in a malpractice suit. That's a very persuasive combination of reasons not to bother with a suit in the first place.

A better recourse for clients who have been cheated by lawyers are client security funds. These funds are financed by dues paid by lawyers through the state bar associations and are designed to reimburse clients who've lost money through their attorneys' misconduct. Most states (with the exception of Utah and Wisconsin) run these funds, but the level of reimbursement varies considerably from one to another. Most claims are settled for about $5,000, but a few result in awards of $200,000 or more.

Don't be surprised if you've never heard of these funds. Bar associations don't publicize their existence very actively for an obvious reason: The funds aren't large enough to compensate all of the clients who think they've been ripped off by a lawyer. "Our fund has been around since 1962," says an official of the New York State Bar Association, "but we don't publicize its existence for fear that its limited resources will be overwhelmed by claims. Even without publicity, claims have been rising sharply in the last few years."

Despite the relative secrecy surrounding them, most funds are active and accessible. The New Jersey Bar Association's Fund, for example, paid out $2.5 million in 1980, according to a trustee report. The largest single amount paid out was $429,478 to 89 clients of a Passaic lawyer who was charged with forgery, obtaining money under false pretenses, and using a corporation to defraud. In that case, unlike most such cases, the lawyer was sent to jail.

WHEN AND HOW TO SUE FOR MALPRACTICE: A CHECKLIST

A malpractice suit is a serious and complicated undertaking. You should give it careful consideration before going ahead. To help you in that process, here are ten key points to keep in mind as you make your decision and plan your course of action:

- Don't sue just because you lost your case.
- Disregard your lawyer's clean record (if it is clean).
- Don't think you're just being paranoid.
- Don't sue if you have something to hide.
- Don't sign away your right to sue.
- Don't threaten a malpractice suit unless you mean it.
- You have more time to decide whether or not to sue than you used to.
- You can sue any lawyer for malpractice, not just your own.
- Your lawyer can be guilty of malpractice if he represents you too zealously.
- Be sure your lawyer has malpractice insurance.

Don't sue just because you lost your case. Whatever you do, resist the temptation to file a malpractice suit simply because you lost your case. Many experts think that losing is the best indicator of malpractice claims, and it's probably true—although there are no surveys to confirm it—that winners sue their lawyers far less often than losers. "In every case, 50 percent of the clients are going to be unhappy," says one litigator. "Somebody has to lose. Even the client who wins may be dissatisfied because the award wasn't what he expected." A winner, however, has the difficult job of showing that he's been damaged *despite* having won.

Disregard your lawyer's clean record (if it is clean). Don't think just because your attorney has no record of malpractice that he's never been guilty of it. Only a small portion of lawyer improprieties are ever discovered by clients, and of those that are, only about 25 percent reach litigation. Of that 25 percent, more than 95 percent are settled out of court, and in almost all of those cases the settlements are private. Lawyers who settle often demand that the malpractice charges be removed from the records and that the very fact, as well as the substance, of the settlement agreements be kept secret. Although lawyers are required by the Code of Professional Responsibility to report any case of professional misconduct known to them, they seldom do. So, just because a lawyer doesn't have a history of client abuse doesn't mean he hasn't abused clients.

Don't think you're just being paranoid. How common is malpractice? Did your lawyer in fact damage your case or are you just being paranoid? "Every lawyer in the world has let a statute of limitations run out," says attorney Paul Rheingold, "just as every doctor has made mistakes."

Don't sue if you have something to hide. This may seem too obvious to mention, but it's something that many people think about too late. You can't count on all the rules about lawyer-client confidentiality once you've sued your lawyer for malpractice. Although a lawyer is normally bound to preserve a client's confidences, in a malpractice suit all the bets are off. "If a client accuses the lawyer," says Clair Nelson, chairman of the ethics committee of the American Bar Association, "then the lawyer is not obligated to stand there with his arms tied."

Don't sign away your right to sue. Do not at any time for any reason sign any agreement by which you waive or sign off your right to sue your lawyer if his services or his advice are incompetent, negligent, or dishonest. At the first signs of client discontent, some lawyers will agree to be more careful if the client will agree not to sue for malpractice. There is some doubt whether such agreements are enforceable, but don't take any chances. Your right to sue for malpractice is a crucial one and you shouldn't surrender it under any circumstances.

Don't threaten a malpractice suit unless you mean it. You could seriously jeopardize your own case by prematurely threatening your lawyer with a malpractice suit. You may put yourself into a position where you *have* to discharge him because the threat of a suit has forced him into a corner, where the only thing for him to do—short of withdrawing—is to practice "defensive law," a process described by legal commentator Lael Scott as "analogous to the doctor who is certain of his diagnosis but, being leery of a potential malpractice suit, will order every test and X-ray in the books for his patient."

You have more time to decide whether or not to sue than you used to. It used to be that you could bring a malpractice suit only within a certain length of time (one or two years) after the attorney's misconduct. If you didn't learn about the actions or didn't realize they had damaged you until after that time, you were out of luck. Although that's still the case in some jurisdictions, in many others, the time period doesn't start until a client actually suffers substantial damage or until the client actually discovers the negligent act. Under the new rule, if you lose a case or are damaged in some other way because of something your attorney did wrong several years ago (say, for example, he wrote a faulty will), you can still sue him.

You can sue any lawyer for malpractice, not just your own. It used to be that you and only you could sue your lawyer for malpractice relating to your business with him. In some jurisdictions, the rule has changed so that anybody damaged by your lawyer's incompetence, negligence, or dishonesty can bring a malpractice suit. That means that if somebody *else's* lawyer is negligent, you can sue him. In the example of the will above, for instance, if you were a beneficiary, you could still sue the lawyer for a negligently prepared will, even if you were not his client.

Your lawyer can be guilty of malpractice if he represents you too zealously. If you have reason to believe that your lawyer is being "overzealous" in your behalf (for example, bribing a witness), we recommend strongly that you discharge him immediately and bring disciplinary action against him. That may be a hard pill to swallow—especially if he's winning the case for you— but there's a distinct possibility that you might be criminally liable if you know of his activity and do nothing about it. Also, now that other people can sue your lawyer, you might also be liable jointly for the damages to your opponent's rights which the lawyer's activities cause. Besides, do you really want a dishonest lawyer representing you?

Be sure your lawyer has malpractice insurance. As the number of malpractice suits has risen, malpractice insurance has become more expensive and harder to secure. Therefore, fewer and fewer lawyers are covered. Some can't afford the higher premiums, others are rejected by the insurers as "high risk." You should avoid this last category altogether. By definition, they're the group most likely to commit malpractice. You should always inquire whether a lawyer carries malpractice insurance—and how much—*before* you hire him. If a dispute arises, you'll be glad you did.

WHAT ARE YOUR CHANCES OF SUCCESS?

Experts estimate that only about one fourth of malpractice claims result in the lawyer paying the client for damages. That may seem like bad odds; in fact, they're relatively encouraging when you consider that less than 1 percent of all arrests result in a conviction.

The other encouraging news is that of that one fourth, almost all are settled out of court. That is, the lawyer pays the client in exchange for dropping the malpractice claim. The advantage to the lawyer is obvious: No trial means no public record, no blemish on his career, no professional embarrassment, and no obstacle to future clients. "In these cases," says New York malpractice lawyer Paul Rheingold, "there's an even greater impetus to settle [than in most cases] because an open court case could affect the lawyer's reputation."

The lawyer's desire to avoid a trial is also a bargaining chip in the hands of the disgruntled client. It means that if you can find a lawyer to file the appropriate papers, if you can get the suit "off the ground" and make it a credible threat, if you can make the prospect of a trial real and immediate, then your chances of realizing some money are very good.

Once a settlement is proposed, there are other bargaining chips on the client's side of the table. Many lawyers will try to get the client to retract the malpractice charges and to agree that the records of the proceedings and the settlement agreement itself will be closed to the public and press. The obvious purpose is to insure that the record won't be available to any client who might want to sue him in the future. Knowing that the lawyer wants these stipulations and why should help you negotiate a more favorable financial arrangement.

If your case does happen to be one of the rare ones that goes to trial, you can take heart in the fact that juries are generally more willing to rule in favor of a client suing a lawyer than a patient suing a doctor. "In 75 to 85 percent of jury verdicts in medical malpractice cases the doctor prevails," says prominent California malpractice lawyer Ed Freidberg, "but I expect in legal negligence cases, it will be the reverse, 85 percent of the jury verdicts will be for the plaintiff."

Index